The International
Airline Industry

The International Airline Industry

Trends, Issues, and Challenges

Nawal K. Taneja
The Ohio State University

Lexington Books
D.C. Heath and Company/Lexington, Massachusetts/Toronto

Cover design by Grace Greczanik.
Front and back cover photo courtesy of ABC International.

Library of Congress Cataloging-in-Publication Data

Taneja, Nawal K.
  The international airline industry.

  Bibliography: p.
  Includes index.
  1. Aeronautics, Commercial.   2. Aeronautics,
Commercial—United States.   3. Airlines.   4. Airlines—
United States.   I. Title.
HE9776.T363   1988   387.7   87-45227
ISBN 0-669-16167-5 (alk. paper)

Published simultaneously in Canada
Printed in the United States of America
Casebound International Standard Book Number: 0-669-16167-5
Library of Congress Catalog Card Number: 87-45227

The paper used in this publication meets the minimum requirements of American National
Standard for Information Sciences—Permanence of Paper for Printed Library Materials,
ANSI Z39.48-1984. ∞™

88 89 90 91 92 8 7 6 5 4 3 2 1

To my mother and father,
Shanti Devi and Dharam Pal

Contents

Figures

Tables

Preface

In recent years, the international airline industry has been going through major structural and operational changes as a result of several factors:

- A rising global interest in the free enterprise system as a means of obtaining faster economic and social development;
- The Pacific gaining on the Atlantic as a center of economic might;
- Consumer demands, at least in the more mature markets, for lower fares and broader price/service options;
- Deregulation of the U.S. airline industry and mounting pressure, directly or indirectly, for more liberalization in international markets;
- Automated systems, which are being used to reduce operating costs (in capacity planning, for example) and to enhance revenues through the use of more effective yield management techniques;
- The privatization trend affecting many government-owned enterprises;
- Technological advances in the airplane, such as greater nonstop range, two-engine operations on the North Atlantic, and more cost-effective turboprops;
- Limiting infrastructural constraints (such as insufficient airport capacity at a number of airports around the world), which may seriously undermine the establishment of a more competitive system; and
- Pending noise regulations, which are forcing airlines based in less developed countries to choose either expensive fleet modernizations or extensive rerouting.

This book examines the direction and degree of change in the international airline industry and the potential implications of these changes with respect to the industry's market structure, performance, and conduct; and the requisite managerial decisions that will have to be made by individual airlines and their respective governments. This book will be of interest to three groups: (1) those directly involved with the regulation, management, and operation of international airlines; (2) those engaged in related endeavors, such as airplane manufacturers, airport owners and operators, and travel agents; and (3) those with an academic interest and some background in this dynamic, stimulating, and challenging industry.

This book is organized into seven chapters, six of which are based on regional definitions of international travel markets (a collection of nations with similar attributes) established by the International Civil Aviation Organization (ICAO). Except for the first chapter, each regional chapter begins with a brief overview of the social, political, economic, geographic, and demographic characteristics of the region that have a direct bearing on air transportation in that area. The remainder of each chapter is devoted—to the extent that data are available—to a description of the region's air transportation market, traffic patterns, and fares; carriers' financial performance; and the future prospects for the carriers based in the region. The first chapter, which deals with North America, follows a different format. It focuses on the major impacts of U.S. deregulation and the development of megacarriers, which are expected to have a chain reaction, forcing marketplace reforms, to varying degrees, in the other five regions of the world. The concluding chapter highlights the need for governments and airline managements to formulate, develop, and implement cost-effective policies and strategies to adapt to the recent developments and emerging trends affecting the airlines.

Acknowledgments

There are many organizations and people to thank for their help, encouragement, and criticism: the Department of Aviation, The Ohio State University; Chris Lyle, Chief-Air Carrier Tariffs, and Richard Smithies, Economist-Air Transport Studies, of the International Civil Aviation Organization's Air Transport Bureau; Richard Nyaga, Head of Government and Industry Affairs, and Geo Besse, Director of Government Affairs, at the International Air Transport Association; Thomas Craig, Director of Market Research at the Boeing Commercial Airplane Company; Kees Veenstra, General Manager of Aeropolitical Affairs at the Association of European Airlines; Wesley Kaldahl, Senior Vice President-International, and Barry Clark, Manager-Route Strategy, at American Airlines; and Abdulaziz Alhazmi, General Manager-Planning and Research, and Shawgi Mushtag, General Manager-Marketing Training, at Saudi Arabian Airlines. I extend special thanks to John B. Fisher, a doctoral student at OSU, for reading and commenting on the entire manuscript several times; Judith Schaeffer, for editing the manuscript; and the staff at Lexington Books. Finally, I thank Yvonne Holsinger, Graphic Supervisor at the OSU Office of Learning Resources, for drawing the regional maps. It should be noted that international boundaries shown on these maps do not imply any official endorsement. Their sole purpose is to provide the reader with a general review of the area under discussion with respect to the development of international air transportation services.

The International
Airline Industry

1
North America

The most dramatic changes in international commercial air transportation during the past ten years have taken place in North American domestic markets (Canada and the United States) as a result of liberalization of government control. The resultant changes include the expansion of hub-and-spoke systems, fare wars, consolidation, code sharing, and greater reliance on automation. Although most of these changes have taken place in the U.S. domestic markets, they have had a profound effect not only on the North American international airline industry but also, to varying degrees, on the worldwide airline industry. Outside this region, pressure to follow the U.S. experience has come from the U.S. government, which has attempted to export its regulatory philosophy, and from consumer groups within each country. In markets outside the United States, airline consumers have been exposed to extensive foreign media coverage of the U.S. deregulation experience, which generally has emphasized the positive aspects of deregulation (such as fare wars, new entrants, and broader price/service options) while ignoring some of the negative aspects (such as increasing delays, fare subsidization, new barriers to entry, and poorer overall service). This chapter examines developments and trends in the North American airline industry as a backdrop to an examination of the degree to which these trends could influence the airline industry in other regions of the world.

The Impact of Deregulation

Until 1978, in both Canada and the United States, all economic aspects of the airline industry had been regulated by federal governments since before World War II. In the United States, the Civil Aeronautics Board (and in Canada, the Canadian Transport Commission) controlled entry and exit and established fares by fixed formulas. By the mid-1970s, civil aviation policy in the United States began to shift in favor of less government involvement, on the premise that tight government control had led to inefficient operations by the airlines and high fares for the public. In October 1978, the U.S. Congress enacted the Airline Deregulation Act of 1978, which placed maximum reliance on competitive market forces to determine the quality, quantity, and price of air transportation services to be provided by the airlines. Government control of entry, exit, fares, and service was phased out gradually over a number of years. The act even provided for termination of the industry's economic regulatory body, the Civil Aeronautics Board (CAB), at the end of 1984. Responsibility for international aviation was turned over to the Department of Transportation (DOT), which was also given the authority to approve airline mergers.

The Canadian government has also been examining the role of economic regulation of its airline industry since the beginning of this decade and has, in fact, allowed de facto domestic deregulation, although legislation (similar to the U.S. Airline Deregulation Act of 1978) has not yet been enacted (as of this writing). The first signs of deregulation in Canada were seen in 1984, when the government introduced its "freedom to move" policy, which led to (1) the cancellation of the rule that had previously limited competitors to 25 percent of Air Canada's route mileage and (2) the opening of most heavily traveled routes in southern Canada to competition. Full deregulation cannot come until the Parliament enacts legislation (which is expected in the near future). However, the industry has already started going through the changes like those in the United States, but at an accelerated pace. Still, given the geographic characteristics of Canada and the limited size of the Canadian market relative to that of the United States, it is difficult to envision that Canadian airlines and passengers will have all the freedoms of their U.S. counterparts. On the other hand, the Canadian carriers will be under less competitive pressure, and service standards should remain high.

The deregulated marketplace is a remarkable contrast to the regulated environment, in which routes, tariffs, service standards, and mergers were strictly controlled by the federal government. Airlines in the United States are now free to charge any fares they want, to enter and exit markets without notice, and to offer virtually any services they please. In addition, mergers and route exchanges have been virtually unchallenged, even when there has been a reduction in competition, as evidenced by DOT's approval of the Republic–Northwest and TWA–Ozark mergers and the transfer of Pan American's trans-Pacific routes to United Airlines. As a quid pro quo for independence, the airlines have given up the protective coverage of the federal government. Market forces now determine an airline's financial fate, and there is no longer any guarantee that an airline will be in service to honor a passenger's advance ticket purchase.

The freedom to exercise managerial initiative has been the greatest single benefit of deregulation from the airlines' point of view. They have been able to experiment with (1) new routes, fares, and services, as demonstrated by the development of hub-and-spoke networks; (2) very low fares during times when the demand for air travel is traditionally low; (3) increased utilization of automation as a competitive tool; (4) "frequent flyer" programs; (5) management techniques and labor policies that are used commonly in other industries; and (6) partnerships with regional carriers, using a common code. These strategies reflect a postderegulation shift in management focus. Carriers in the United States no longer compete on a service basis under a regulated price umbrella; rather, the pressure of a free market forces them to become "bottom line"–oriented.

For example, the expansion of hub-and-spoke systems has been a significant operational development of the managerial freedom gained from deregulation. Although such systems had been operated on a limited basis by a few carriers prior to deregulation, after 1978 every major airline in the United States quickly added new hubs and expanded operations at existing hubs. Initially, the established higher-cost carriers viewed hub development as a strategy to buy time in which to change their cost structures. A sound feeder network into a strong hub reduced competition for the incumbent carrier, since a minute percentage of all city pairs have sufficient traffic to support nonstop service. Subsequently, the incumbents began to recognize the tremendous traffic synergies of a hub-and-spoke system with respect to an increase in market coverage, a more effective control of the traffic, and a decrease in the dependence on other carriers for connecting traffic. Moreover, hub-and-spoke systems allowed airlines to achieve greater efficiencies in their operations. In Canada, the development of hub-and-spoke systems has been limited by the fact that more than three-quarters of the population lives in a 100-mile-wide corridor along the U.S. border. Consequently, although it is possible to develop hubs to transport traffic between eastern and western Canadian cities, there is very limited potential for north–south connections, unless they involve cities in the United States.

For passengers, the development of the hub-and-spoke systems under deregulation has provided some advantages and some disadvantages. On the positive side, hubs have increased the amount of intraline service available in lightly traveled point-to-point markets. On the negative side, nonstop service has been reduced in many markets, more passengers have experienced increased circuity and longer travel times, delays have been commonplace because of hub structure, more connecting flights have meant added inconvenience because of equipment changes, and many airports are severely congested at peak periods.

Since deregulation, the level of service in smaller communities has undergone rapid change. Some small cities have been dropped, some have been added, and most have experienced a replacement in service. When a major carrier has left, jet service out of a small community has often been replaced by a regional carrier using a much smaller airplane. Moreover, the historically high turnover among regional carriers has increased uncertainty about reliability of service. The change in air service in many small communities has caused some concern about their ability to maintain their economic bases and to attract new businesses. Now more than ever, air service has become a high-priority item in business location decisions. In Canada, service to northern communities continues to be regulated to ensure continuity. It is important to keep in mind that the percentage of low-density markets is much higher in Canada than in the United States. Thus, it is expected that a much larger number of commuter carriers will be formed in Canada, with the result of less jet service (but higher frequency) in the low-density markets.

Without a doubt, the most widely publicized result of deregulation has been the introduction of extremely low fares in selected markets and more innovative marketing of air transportation services. After a brief adjustment period immediately following deregulation, the low fares introduced by new entrants generally have been matched by the incumbent carriers on a capacity-control basis or with certain restrictions. However, along with lower fares in some markets, there have been higher fares in other markets. Also, although the average percentage discount from normal economy fares and the percentage of passengers traveling on discount fares have increased since deregulation, the average real fare has not changed so dramatically. The number of discount fares available and the amount of discount available have both increased significantly, but so have the normal economy fares on which the discounts are based.

Deregulation has given rise to some well-publicized promotional fares, but fare disparities between markets of similar distance have never been greater. Prior to deregulation, the Civil Aeronautics Board approved fares that subsidized service in short-haul markets from profits in long-haul markets. After deregulation, the practice of cross-subsidization appears to have shifted from markets of different distances to markets with different levels of competition. In recent years, fare levels in individual markets have been a function of the absence or presence of a strong discount carrier rather than just the total number of carriers.

Although air travel in some U.S. domestic markets has become less expensive, it has become more difficult for all segments. It has been reported that 90 percent of the passengers are able to use a discount that averages about 60 percent. However, not only are discounts applied to a much higher normal economy fare, but to get these discounts, travelers must go at the carrier's convenience and cannot change their plans without substantial penalty. To offer low fares, airlines have had to cut back on services, which has resulted in long lines, lost baggage, busy reservation lines, and lower overall quality.

In the years immediately following deregulation, the established carriers were still operating with labor contracts negotiated during the regulated era, whereas the new entrants began operations with much lower paid nonunion employees. Recognizing that labor costs are, by far, the largest controllable cost in the airline industry, the incumbent carriers began to implement strategies to cut labor costs. Revised work rules, two-tier wage scales, voluntary bankruptcies, furloughs, enhanced profit sharing, and establishment of nonunionized subsidiaries have been among the tactics adopted to reduce unit labor costs. The reduced labor costs of the U.S. carriers have affected U.S. domestic and international operations. If airline consumers have been the big winners from deregulation, then airline employees have been the big losers. In the case of Canadian airlines, labor costs have been decreasing more because of the increase in labor productivity than because of any significant reduction in wages.

Because of lower operating costs, a number of new carriers entered the marketplace with alternative price-service options. Most new carriers elected to compete with low fares, offering a different product in the marketplace. Following are just five examples of the differences in the product offered by one of the largest low-fare new entrants, People Express. First, the airline provided one-class service, with high-density seating on each aircraft, resulting in considerably less room per passenger. Second, the airline's simplistic reservation system caused some difficulty in accessing its services. Third, high fleet utilization forced the airline to schedule tight turnarounds, increasing the probability of missed connections and the buildup of delays throughout the system. Fourth, the airline unbundled the traditional product and began charging for services that traditionally had been included in the price of a ticket—for example, passenger baggage checking and cabin food service. Fifth, higher load factors were achieved in part through a higher overbooking policy, which increased the percentage of passengers bumped from flights on which they were holding confirmed space.

The discount airlines' lower costs can thus be explained by these product differences (along with the use of used airplanes and nonunion labor). However, it is also important to keep in mind that these product differences existed because (1) the new entrants were free to offer product/service options that the incumbents had not been allowed to offer while under control of the CAB; and (2) the established carriers needed time to adjust their routes, fleets, and labor contracts to compete more effectively with the new entrants. Despite the awkward beginning, established carriers have finally been able to reconfigure their resources, not only to counter the competitive threat of new entrants but also to compete effectively among themselves and with other foreign carriers. Computerized reservation systems, attractive frequent flyer programs, nationwide route networks, significantly lower operating costs, better fleet alignment, code-sharing agreements with feeder regional airlines, and mergers and acquisitions have enabled many of the stronger incumbents to reassert themselves.

Finally, deregulation has been responsible, to a large extent, for straining the capacity of the infrastructure facilities, particularly the capacity of airports and airways. Between 1979 and 1983, airplane departures in the United States declined by about 10 percent as a result of three factors: (1) an increase in the price of fuel; (2) a severe economic recession; and (3) the strike by the Professional Air Traffic Controllers Organization (PATCO). Since 1983, airplane departures have been steadily increasing; at the beginning of 1987, they were about 30 percent above the 1984 level. The increase in departures, coupled with the increase in hub-and-spoke activity, has led to an increase in airplane and passenger delays. Typical estimates of the costs of delays are $2 billion per year to the airlines and $1 billion per year in lost passenger time.

Unfortunately, the capacity of airports and the air traffic control system has not kept pace with the increase in aviation activity, partly as a result of the insufficient funds released from the Aviation Trust Fund, which is estimated to contain a surplus of more than $4 billion. Although approximately two-thirds of the delays are weather-related, some observers claim that funds released from the Trust Fund could be used to conduct research and development that could reduce weather-related delays. The Congress has not seen fit to release the surplus funds, however, presumably because it would make the U.S. federal budget deficit look even worse. Hence, the U.S. federal government continues to control two integral components of air transportation—the airports and the air traffic control system—either directly (for example, through slot allocations) or indirectly (through control over the Aviation Trust Fund). Consequently, the airlines are the only component left to the forces of the marketplace.

Airport and airway congestion and the resulting delays are not just added expenses for the airlines and nuisances for passengers; they have become obstacles to deregulation working according to forces of the marketplace. Some attempts have been made to allow the forces of the free market to allocate the scarce resources at congested airports—for example, the purchase and sale of airport slots according to the forces of the marketplace. However, such a system inevitably finds infrastructure facilities controlled by the airlines that have the greatest resources. Any effort to set aside a certain percentage of slots for small carriers with limited resources runs counter to the free market theory.

The airlines are also proposing the establishment of an air traffic control corporation, which would be owned by the government but would operate according to commercial criteria and practices. Regrettably, most of the actions that have been taken, expected, or suggested (for example, restructured pricing policies, proliferation of slot-controlled airports, increased use of alternate airports, and implementation of the East Coast Plan) represent short-

Table 1–1
IATA International On-Flight Origin and Destination Traffic Statistics for North America, 1985

Region Pair	Passengers (000), Both Directions	Percentage of World Total
North America–Middle America	9,739	6.0
North America–South America	2,622	1.6
North America–Middle East	852	0.5
North America–Europe	17,881	11.0
North America–Africa	325	0.2
North America–Far East	3,483	2.1
North America–Southwest Pacific	1,170	0.7
Within North America	5,650	3.5
Subtotal	41,722	25.6
World total	162,418	100.0

Source: International Air Transport Association (IATA), *World Air Transport Statistics, 1985* (Geneva: IATA, June 1986).

term solutions to the airport and airway problem. The only long-term solution is to build more airports and expand existing airports. Unfortunately, it is highly unlikely that the public would allow the implementation of this solution, given the very strong opposition to further development for environmental reasons, particularly noise pollution.

The Air Transportation System

Because of North America's relative wealth, large population base, and sizable land area, its air transportation system is the most developed in the world. In 1985, the airlines based in this region accounted for 38.5 percent of the world's total scheduled ton-kilometers. In terms of international activity, the North American region ranks second, behind Europe, with 19.9 percent of the total activity. Both the share of total traffic and the share of international traffic have been declining during the past ten years, primarily as a result of the gain in share of the traffic captured by the airlines based in the Asia-Pacific region.

Although all major U.S. airlines provide some international air transportation services, the dominant airlines are Pan American, TWA, Northwest, and United (which acquired Pan American's Pacific routes). In Canada, the majority of international services are provided by Air Canada and Canadian Pacific (now called Canadian Airlines). Table 1–1 shows the relative sizes of

Table 1–2
Passenger Travel between the United States and the Top Fifty Destinations, 1986

Country	Total Passengers (000)	% U.S. Citizen	Percent U.S.-Flag Carriers	Charter as % of Total
United Kingdom	6,278	57	53	3
Mexico	5,618	76	42	4
Japan	5,011	32	47	2
Bahamas	3,692	77	74	17
West Germany	3,140	59	48	8
France	1,775	51	59	7
Jamaica	1,624	78	40	12
Dominican Republic	1,301	80	60	2
Netherlands	1,139	54	9	4
Italy	979	58	48	1
South Korea	921	58	23	1
Bermuda	894	94	95	4
Netherlands Antilles	870	83	78	15
Switzerland	832	59	26	10
Brazil	828	43	47	5
Scandinavia	772	46	22	1
Spain	604	63	34	7
Belgium	600	63	51	1
Australia	587	52	33	0
Hong Kong	570	72	60	0
Ireland	564	68	36	3
Colombia	549	49	39	0
Venezuela	508	44	55	0
China/Taiwan	467	57	17	0
Barbados	428	81	75	5
Israel	423	66	32	2
New Zealand	387	46	47	0
Panama Republic	377	61	70	0
Grand Cayman	371	76	27	6
Haiti	340	59	82	1
Philippines	319	74	31	0
Guatemala	308	47	45	1
Costa Rica	297	58	39	1
Argentina	287	37	59	1
Antigua	260	80	60	4
French Polynesia	247	70	30	28

Table 1–2 continued

Country	Total Passengers (000)	% U.S. Citizen	Percent U.S.-Flag Carriers	Charter as % of Total
Ecuador	244	53	42	0
Portugal	238	77	44	16
Mariana Islands	231	42	91	0
Fiji Islands	227	62	20	0
Honduras	215	51	20	0
El Salvador	197	49	12	1
Iceland	184	66	1	2
Trinidad/Tobago	177	52	37	2
Greece	177	68	21	3
India	152	62	16	0
Yugoslavia	118	61	1	4
Finland	118	52	0	2
Chile	107	44	44	1
Virgin Islands (U.K.)	107	84	28	1
Total	46,662	61	48	5

Source: Data provided by the U.S. Department of Transportation.

intercontinental markets to and from North America. As a whole, the North American region accounts for about one-fourth of the total international passenger travel. The data include both scheduled and charter traffic. North America–Europe is the largest single market outside the intra-European market. During 1985, almost 18 million passengers (11 percent of total world passenger traffic) traveled between North America and Europe. Despite its high growth in the last decade, the market between North America and the Far East is still considerably smaller than the North Atlantic market. The second largest market, after North America–Europe, is between North America and Middle America, which includes Central America and the Caribbean.

Table 1–2 shows the volume of passenger travel between the United States and the top fifty destinations in 1986. A total of 47 million passengers traveled between the United States and those fifty countries. Table 1–2, compiled from data reported by the Department of Transportation, does not include air travel between the United States and Canada, which is estimated to be 10 million passengers per year.[1] Of the top five destinations, two are in Europe (the United Kingdom and West Germany), two are in the Latin America and Caribbean region (Mexico and Bahamas), and one is in the Asia-Pacific region (Japan). With the exception of a few Caribbean islands, Portugal, and Switzerland, charter traffic accounts for an insignificant proportion of the total travel. Of the total passenger traffic between the United

States and these fifty countries, 61 percent of the passengers were U.S. citizens, but U.S.-flag carriers transported only 48 percent of the total traffic. Although, on the average, the U.S.-flag carriers transport almost half of the total passenger traffic, their share is only 9 percent of the traffic to and from the Netherlands, the ninth largest destination from the United States. Other markets in which the U.S.-flag share is less than 10 percent are Iceland, Yugoslavia, and Finland. Indeed, in thirty-nine of the top fifty markets, the percentage of traffic carried by the U.S.-flag carriers is less than the percentage of U.S. travelers in the market.

The North Atlantic market is not only the largest intercontinental market; it is also the most competitive international market in the world. At the end of 1986, thirteen carriers from North America (ten from the United States and three from Canada) and twenty two carriers from Europe provided passenger service on the North Atlantic. Carriers based in other regions of the world—such as the Middle East, Africa, and Asia-Pacific—also provided service on the North Atlantic. The diversity of carriers and the procompetitive attitude of the U.S. government (and now Canada) have kept passenger fares at low levels relative to the world average and have led to the introduction of a broad spectrum of price/service options. Figure 1–1 illustrates the history of the average North Atlantic economy passenger fare relative to the value of the consumer price index. Since 1980, the average economy fare has been increasing at a lower rate than the consumer price index. Figure 1–2 shows the distribution of North Atlantic passenger traffic by fare type. The proliferation of discount fares is clearly evident from these data. For example, the excursion capacity-controlled fares accounted for only 6.8 percent of the total traffic in 1975. Ten years later, they accounted for 51.9 percent of the total traffic.

Prior to the signing of the liberal bilateral agreements between the United States and the growing Pacific countries (Korea, Malaysia, Singapore, and Taiwan), fares in the trans-Pacific markets had been high relative to the world average, in part because of the protective attitudes of major countries such as Japan and Australia. A number of the smaller airlines that operated outside the IATA fare conference machinery could have implemented lower fares if they had had the route authority to serve trans-Pacific markets. Now the proliferation of the lower-cost airlines in the trans-Pacific markets and the changing attitudes of the Australian and, to some extent, Japanese governments are leading to fare wars on the Pacific. There is one major difference, however, between the trans-Atlantic and the trans-Pacific fare wars. In the trans-Pacific markets, the major beneficiaries of fare wars have been the travel agents. Faced with overcapacity, the airlines' desperate efforts to sell seats have led to commission rates approaching 40 percent.

The competitive situation on the Pacific is expected to intensify further as a result of the Memorandum of Understanding between the United States

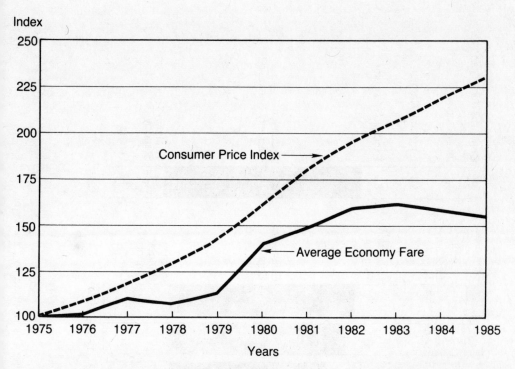

Source: International Air Transport Association (IATA), *World Air Transport Statistics, 1985* (Geneva: IATA, June 1986), 36.

Figure 1–1. Comparison of North Atlantic Fares and the Consumer Price Index

and Japan signed on May 1, 1985. During August 1985, a peak travel month, three U.S. carriers and eight foreign carriers offered scheduled service between the United States and Japan (185 flights per week). Since then, United has replaced Pan American, and three additional scheduled airlines have been authorized to provide scheduled passenger service—two from the United States and one from Japan. Competition is expected to increase substantially, not only because of the increase in the number of carriers but also because of the strength of the new carriers. United is a far more formidable competitor than Pan American was, given its domestic feed, its financial resources, and its computerized reservation system. Northwest, which already had a major hub at Tokyo, now serves nine points beyond Tokyo. In addition, Northwest has acquired Republic to improve its domestic feed and has a share in TWA's computerized reservation system. These acquisitions will make Northwest a more powerful competitor in the domestic and international marketplace.

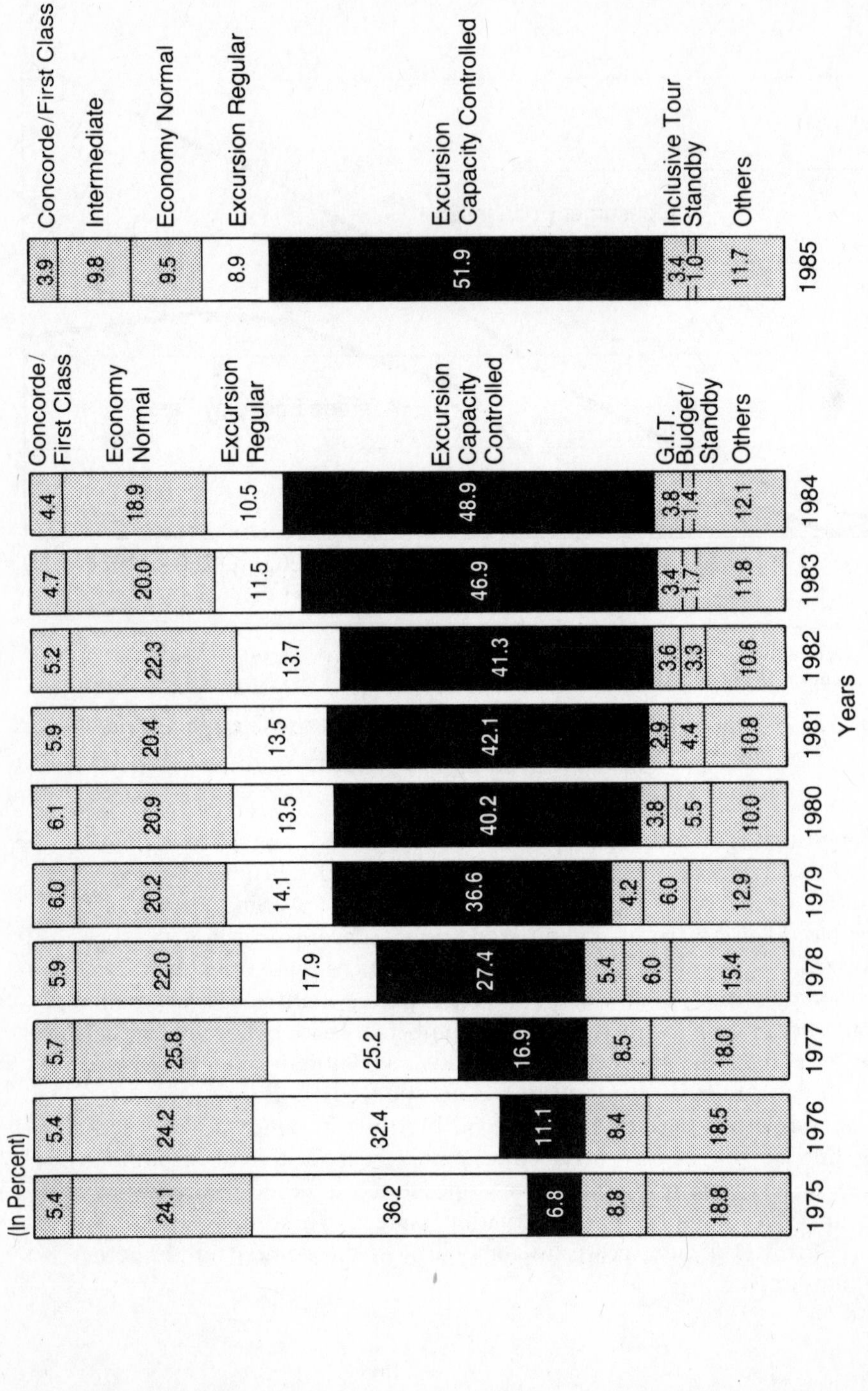

(In Percent)	1975	1976	1977	1978	1979	1980	1981	1982	1983	1984
Concorde/First Class	5.4	5.4	5.7	5.9	6.0	6.1	5.9	5.2	4.7	4.4
Economy Normal	24.1	24.2	25.8	22.0	20.2	20.9	20.4	22.3	20.0	18.9
Excursion Regular	36.2	32.4	25.2	17.9	14.1	13.5	13.5	13.7	11.5	10.5
Excursion Capacity Controlled	6.8	11.1	16.9	27.4	36.6	40.2	42.1	41.3	46.9	48.9
G.I.T.	8.8	8.4	8.5	5.4	4.2	3.8	2.9	3.6	3.4	3.8
Budget/Standby				6.0	6.0	5.5	4.4	3.3	1.7	1.4
Others	18.8	18.5	18.0	15.4	12.9	10.0	10.8	10.6	11.8	12.1

	1985
Concorde/First Class	3.9
Intermediate	9.8
Economy Normal	9.5
Excursion Regular	8.9
Excursion Capacity Controlled	51.9
Inclusive Tour	3.4
Standby	1.0
Others	11.7

Years

Source: International Air Transport Association (IATA), World Air Transport Statistics, 1985 (Geneva: IATA, June 1986), 36.

Figure 1–2. North Atlantic Passenger Distribution by Fare Type

The financial performance of the international carriers based in North America has been sporadic during the past ten years. The following observations summarize the recent performance of the industry. First, the industry as a whole has reported poor profit margins relative to those of other industries. Second, the profit margin has varied significantly within the industry. During the first nine months of 1986, five carriers posted net incomes ranging from about $50 million to about $200 million, while four other carriers reported net losses ranging from about $50 million to more than $300 million. As a group, these nine carriers, which represent about 95 percent of the total passenger traffic (measured in revenue passenger miles), reported a net loss in excess of $300 million during the first nine months of 1986. Third, the financial performance of the industry during the past two years was relatively poor, despite declining labor costs, fuel prices, and interest rates. Fourth, it is important to examine the sources of profit for the carriers that are profitable. The computerized reservation system of American Airlines, for example, has been responsible for a large percentage of the company's net profit.

In the area of labor costs, the trend of declining costs seems to have bottomed out. The level of B-scale rates has begun to increase, as exemplified by American's recent negotiations; also, the industry has begun to accept parity between six and ten years. Since there is direct competition between the rates paid by low-cost airlines and B-rates at the larger airlines, an increase in B-rates has led to increases in labor rates at the low-cost airlines. In addition, labor costs of low-cost airlines have begun to increase as personnel gain seniority. The trend is evident even at Continental, which has just announced raises as high as 20 percent for its pilots.

Airlines are expecting that a severe shortage of pilots will develop within the next few years as a result of (1) growth in the airline industry (more airlines, more routes, and higher utilization of fleet) and (2) a decline in the number of pilots supplied by the military. The latter results from military manpower reductions to peacetime levels; the military's attempt to retain as many of its pilots as possible, given the high cost of training; and the existence of B-scale wages, which make it less attractive for military pilots to join the civilian workforce. This shortage will be made up from the smaller and less financially secure airlines that cannot pay as well as the larger airlines, which also offer greater benefits and glamour. There is concern, however, that some airlines have begun to reduce the qualifications for their pilot aspirants.

Although airline costs will continue to depend on external factors—such as the supply of pilots, the price of fuel, and the level of interest rates—the general consensus in the industry is that once the consolidation process is complete, the resultant megacarriers will be financially stronger and better positioned to generate returns closer to the risks involved. This hypothesis seems plausible in light of the attributes of megacarriers discussed in the next section.

Development of Survival Attributes

The prevailing attitude in the North American airline industry is that to prosper in the new marketplace, a carrier has one of three choices: (1) become a megacarrier; (2) become a feeder to a megacarrier; or (3) fill a small but well-defined niche in the marketplace. The major airlines in the United States and Canada have chosen the first strategy and either have become or are taking the necessary steps to become megacarriers. To be successful megacarriers, the U.S. airlines have been attempting to develop the following five attributes: (1) a large national and international route network; (2) a sufficient number of strategically located hubs with cost-effective feeder systems; (3) labor agreements that provide low costs and high productivity in the long run; (4) an in-house automation system to provide computerized reservations and the necessary analytical capability to manage yield and capacity cost-effectively; and (5) an attractive frequent flyer program. Some of these attributes are interdependent. For example, one attractive feature of a frequent flyer program is the availability of a national and international network of routes on which passengers can cash in their bonus miles. Similarly, the value of a hub-and-spoke system increases with an increase in the number of spokes. An increase in the number of spokes leads, in turn, to the development of national and eventually international coverage.

Since deregulation, major U.S. carriers have been attempting to acquire the attributes of megacarriers either through internal development or through the merger-acquisition process. Examples of internal changes include the development of new hubs, such as American's at Nashville, Raleigh-Durham, and San Juan. Examples of external developments include the merger-acquisition activity typified by United's purchase of Pan American's Pacific routes and Northwest's acquisition of 50 percent of TWA's PARS computerized reservation system. All carriers have been strengthening their traffic feed at their hubs by increasing their own flights, by making arrangements with other carriers to provide the traffic feed (as in the case of TWA and Piedmont in New York), or by either acquiring regional carriers or using code-sharing arrangements.

Megacarriers consider their market share of the industry to be an important characteristic of power. Table 1–3 shows the consolidated market share of eight U.S. airlines, based on their operations during the first quarter of 1986 and for the entire twelve months of 1986. At the end of the first quarter of 1986, these eight U.S. airlines captured 67 percent of the total market. During the next nine months, there was a massive consolidation such that, by year end, these eight airlines accounted for 92 percent of the total market (measured in revenue passenger miles). The largest change in market share was achieved by Texas Air, whose market share increased from 5.5 percent to 19.5 percent, taking into account all its subsidiaries. The recent merger activity reflects the view that in order to compete effectively with the mega-

Table 1–3
Market Share of the Top Eight U.S. Airlines after Mergers
(percentage)

Airline	Market Share[a]	
	1st Quarter 1986	*1986*
Texas Air	5.5	19.5
United	14.5	16.5
American	14.2	13.6
Delta	9.5	11.8
Northwest	6.3	10.0
TWA	6.9	8.3
Pan American	6.7	6.2
USAir	3.0	6.0
All others	33.4	8.1

Source: Data provided by Airline Economics, Inc.
[a]Based on revenue passenger miles.

carriers at the upper end of the spectrum, the carriers at the lower end must either merge their operations or quickly grow internally. Another aspect of size is the total number of destinations served, either directly or through a tie-in with regional carriers. In this context, Texas Air is in a league of its own, with almost 300 destinations; the next largest group (United, American, and Delta) has about 200 destinations each. At the lower end of the spectrum are airlines such as Pan American and TWA, each serving about 100 destinations. At the beginning of 1987, fifteen regional airlines were sharing the common code of Texas Air and accounting for about one-third of the 300 cities served by Texas Air.

The consolidation process has also restructured the airline industry in Canada. Ten years ago, there were three groups of airlines: (1) Air Canada and Canadian Pacific Airlines; (2) five smaller airlines, each confined to a regional territory; and (3) "third-level" airlines connecting small communities to each other and to larger airports. Now there are two large airlines—Air Canada and Canadian Airlines International, which was formed through a merger of Canadian Pacific Airlines and Pacific Western Airlines. Although it is still slightly smaller than Air Canada, Canadian Airlines is expected to become a formidable competitor for Air Canada. These two airlines had previously acquired the other four regional airlines. In addition to the two majors, scheduled service is also provided by Wardair, a former charter airline. More than a dozen regional airlines have sprung up as feeders to either Air Canada or Canadian Airlines.

Until recently, Air Canada has had a monopoly, or close to it, on many of the country's busiest domestic and international routes. For example, Air Canada's competitors were limited to 25 percent of its domestic route mileage. Air Canada obtained a market share of about 60 percent of the domestic and international passenger traffic, which consisted of more than 25 million passengers a year. Now that Air Canada's routes are no longer protected, some observers fear the establishment of a "duopoly," with roughly equivalent cost structures and similar products and only about half a dozen significantly sized markets. However, this is not expected to be the case, partly because of Wardair and partly because Canadian Airlines will undoubtedly offer parallel service with Air Canada to international destinations, such as the eastern United States and the United Kingdom. Air Canada, in turn, is expected to fly the Pacific routes. Although fare wars have not been as extensive in Canada as in the United States, it is reported that service levels have increased even further, as exemplified by Air Canada's highly praised business class service. In summary, although the restructuring process started later in Canada than in the United States, it is finishing there well before it will in the United States. Two reasons that can be cited for this accelerated pace are the timing of the de facto deregulation and the size of the Canadian market. In the United States, deregulation came in the middle of a recession, whereas in Canada it came during a peak in the economic cycle—a time during which a new airline is not likely to enter the marketplace either with the hope of attracting price-sensitive passengers or with the idea of acquiring assets cheaply. Moreover, the smaller size of the Canadian market is not conducive to attracting new entrants of any significant size.

The third aspect of size relates to the number, location, and size of hubs. In terms of number of hubs, Texas Air and American are at one end of the spectrum, with seven and six hubs, respectively, while TWA and Pan American are at the other end of the spectrum, with two and three hubs, respectively. Besides increasing the total number of hubs, each carrier has attempted to select hubs at different locations, to participate in as much of the total national and international market as possible. American's hubs at Nashville and Raleigh-Durham, for example, allow the airline to participate in traffic that could not be carried over its hubs at Dallas or Chicago.

Historically, three U.S. airlines competed for intercontinental traffic: Northwest, Pan American, and TWA. After deregulation, a number of other U.S. major carriers have begun service in intercontinental markets. For example, Texas Air, Northwest, American, and Delta, combined, carry almost as many passengers on the North Atlantic as TWA. Even a relatively small carrier, Piedmont, has been authorized to serve London from its hub at Charlotte. Domestic U.S. airlines that previously did not provide service on the North Atlantic now carry (as a group) almost as many passengers as Pan American and TWA, and their share is increasing. American Airlines trans-

Atlantic passenger traffic increased about 40 percent from 1985 to 1986, whereas the total industry traffic declined about 7 percent during the same period. On the Pacific, Delta and American have now begun service to Japan. United States majors that have begun serving intercontinental markets since deregulation are relying heavily on their strong domestic hubs, not only to compete effectively with foreign-flag carriers but also to compete with the older U.S. international airlines. Compare, for example, the feed available to the international operations of Texas Air and Pan American, as shown in figures 1–3 and 1–4. These two figures clearly show the potential for Texas Air to survive and the difficulties experienced by Pan American because of the lack of sufficient feeder traffic.

A key emerging trend is the increasing utilization of automation in airline marketing, particularly in distribution, pricing, and inventory control. Since the majority of airline tickets are sold through travel agents, each airline attempts to persuade travel agents, through various means, to sell its air transportation services. Travel agents, in turn, use computer terminals to access the inventory of seats available for sale and to make reservations. Major airlines have developed their own computerized reservation systems (for example, American's Sabre and United's Apollo) and have made their own terminals available to travel agents. A travel agent can use one airline's computerized reservation system to access the inventory of another airline, but operational characteristics of each reservation system induce the agent to book on the host airline. Furthermore, the airline whose system is used by a travel agent (the host airline) receives direct and indirect benefits even if the reservation is made on a competitor airline. Host airlines charge co-host airlines handsomely for the privilege of listing their services. Consequently, each owner of a computerized reservation system has attempted to persuade travel agents to use its computer terminals.

As of 1986, American's Sabre system was clearly in the lead in terms of both the number of travel agencies utilizing the system (about 40 percent) and the number of terminals in place (about 35 percent). United's Apollo system has a market share of about 25 percent of travel agents and about 30 percent of the terminals. The remaining three vendors are Texas Air (SystemOne), TWA (PARS), and Delta (DATAS II).[2] Co-host airlines have complained about the level and structure of fees, the biases introduced by host airlines in their systems, and the use of marketing information to gain a competitive advantage. Examples of bias include the favorable manner in which the system owner's flight information is displayed as compared to the display of information on the services offered by competitors. The issue of bias raised such strong complaints that the CAB started an investigation to determine the validity of the allegations. The results of this investigation led the Department of Transportation to establish guidelines for listing competitive services fairly on computer screens. Domestic U.S. airlines were not the

Texas Air Corporation
Merged Hub Services
North America

Source: Airline Economics, Inc.

Figure 1–3. Texas Air Corporation Merged Hub Services, North America

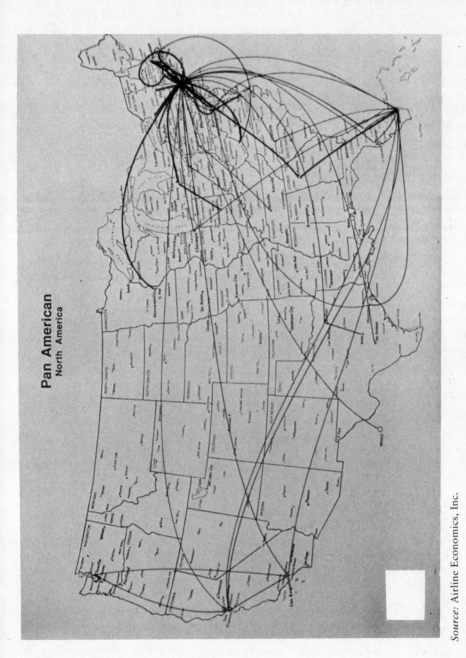

Source: Airline Economics, Inc.

Figure 1–4. Pan American Routes, North America

only airlines to express concerns about bias. Some international airlines felt so strongly about bias in the computerized reservation systems that it became a major issue in a number of bilateral discussions.

Not satisfied with either the regulatory steps taken or the commercial pressures applied to eliminate bias, thirty two airlines took part in discussions aimed at developing an alternative unbiased system. These discussions did not result in any consensus on the optimal direction to follow. As of now, three major U.S. carriers have taken different courses of action. Before it acquired Eastern, Texas Air did not have its own computer reservation system in place at travel agencies. Having acquired Eastern, however, Texas Air became the owner of SystemOne. Northwest decided to acquire a 50 percent interest in TWA's PARS system. And Pan American opted to enter into a marketing agreement with American Airlines that involves the use of American's computerized reservation system as well as a merger of the two airlines' frequent flyer programs. To compete more effectively with the U.S. carriers, the larger European carriers are developing their own computerized reservation systems, exemplified by the recent announcement (by Air France, Iberia, Lufthansa, and SAS) to develop Amadeus.

The second major use of automation by major airlines relates to the management of yield—that is, controlling the number of seats sold at various prices on each flight. The ability to manage yield cost-effectively varies significantly, and airlines that have mastered the technique have been generously rewarded. In fact, major airlines that have implemented sound yield management techniques not only have improved their financial performance but have been able to compete effectively with the lower fares offered by low-cost new entrants. Automation has also helped airlines administer their frequent flyer programs, which have proved to be extremely effective competitive tools in building passenger loyalty.

The strategies implemented by North American megacarriers are proof of the prevailing conviction that the five primary characteristics of megacarriers are essential for survival in the new environment. Among these five characteristics, U.S. airlines consider mass to be the single most important attribute for survival and consider the merger-acquisition process more cost-effective than internal growth as a means for acquiring mass. Furthermore, the U.S. airlines have been able to use this preferred strategy for acquiring mass because of the very permissive attitude of the Reagan administration.

Future Prospects

The first phase of airline deregulation in the United States was characterized by turmoil, bankruptcies, labor confrontations, and major fare wars. The second phase, which is now coming to an end, has been characterized by consolidation, both in the United States and in Canada. The merger-acquisition trend is expected to continue, although to a limited degree among the major carriers as the number of carriers decreases. Consolidation among the regional carriers is likely to increase, however, as a result of the consolidation among the majors. A major issue now being debated is the impact on competition of concentration in the industry and the unlikelihood of the emergence of new low-fare carriers of any significant size. From the evidence available to date, it appears that some benefits of competition will continue to exist, even though they will be less than those achieved in the past and will vary from market to market. Competition among airlines to move passengers over their respective hubs will continue and will keep fares from rising in the medium- and long-haul markets. Fares in short-haul markets (spokes to each carrier's hubs) will continue to be relatively high. Moreover, without the threat of new entrants of significant size, overall fares are likely to increase in proportions equal to or greater than increases in operating costs.

The competitive battle for market share in both the trans-Atlantic and the trans-Pacific markets has begun to take on new dimensions as U.S. megacarriers begin to use feeder traffic and sophisticated computerized reservations systems as competitive weapons and as the Japanese and the Australian governments gradually relax economic controls over their airlines. On the North Atlantic, this situation is likely to prove difficult for the smaller specialist carriers and the financially weaker higher-cost carriers. The end result is likely to accelerate the consolidation process both in North America and in Europe (along the lines of joint operations between Sabena and BCAL initially, followed by actual mergers along the lines proposed between Sabena and SAS). On the Pacific, the consolidation process is less likely to take place, given that there are fewer carriers than there are on the North Atlantic. Moreover, the majority of the carriers based in the Asia-Pacific region can compete effectively with the U.S. megacarriers because of their lower unit operating costs, high labor productivity, marketing flair, and strong control of the home market. In other words, some of the carriers based in the Asia-Pacific region already possess the survival attributes of megacarriers. Competition in the North America–Latin America/Caribbean market is expected to be limited to the Caribbean subregion in the near future for two reasons. First, the Caribbean market is much larger than the South American market. Second, with the exception of one or two countries, such as Chile, the prevailing attitude in the South American countries supports a tightly regulated market environment.

One area of U.S. international aviation policy that continues to concern major foreign airlines and their governments is the issue of cabotage rights in the United States. A number of European nations—and, more recently, Canada—claim that there is a contradiction in U.S. international aviation policy. On the one hand, the U.S. government promotes open skies (unlimited entry); on the other hand, it refuses to give cabotage (internal) traffic rights to foreign airlines. It is highly unlikely that the U.S. government will agree to give cabotage traffic rights in the near future for at least two reasons. First, there is no common stance for or against cabotage either among the U.S. government agencies or among the U.S. airlines. Second, the award of such traffic rights would require a change in the Federal Aviation Act—an unlikely event at this time, given the protectionist trade policies being considered by the U.S. Congress.

Airport and airway congestion represents the most serious obstacle to the future growth of the air transportation industry in the United States. The only feasible long-term solution is the development of new airports and the expansion of existing major airports. This solution is unacceptable to the public, however, because of environmental considerations, particularly noise pollution. Unfortunately, unless means can be found to relieve the public's concern about noise (and ultimately congestion), thereby allowing the government and the industry to proceed with the necessary development of airports, airline reregulation may become a reality.

Notes

1. Western Transportation Advisory Council, "The Canada—U.S. Treaty Is Particularly Important," *WESTAC Newsletter* 12 (October 1986): 13.

2. Nadine Godwin, "Agents Extend Role of In-House Computers," *Travel Weekly,* 22 September 1986, 110.

2
Latin America and the Caribbean

T he financial performance of airlines based in ICAO's Latin America/
Caribbean region depends heavily on the economic and financial
condition of the countries within this region. In the case of the Caribbean-based airlines, it also depends on the state of the U.S. economy. Some
nations are reporting an economic revival. Unfortunately, the economies of
many others remain volatile because of the uncertainties associated with high
levels of external debt and inflation rates. The crushing burden of massive
debt and uncontrollable inflation has created monumental difficulties for the
airlines in managing their assets. For instance, even though the airlines' financial results have been hampered by high costs and excessive debt service
obligations, they must find additional funding for large-scale fleet replace-
ments in order to comply with pending noise regulations. In addition, the
remedial steps many nations have taken to improve their financial status have
had a negative impact on the economic welfare of their people, hence limiting
their propensity to travel in the short term. Moreover, within the region, there
has been a diversion of tourism from high-cost to low-cost destinations. This
chapter analyzes these developments and prospects for the future, highlight-
ing individual countries and groups of countries on the basis of their particular situations.

Economic, Demographic, and Political Characteristics

The ICAO groups the thirty-two nations and the dependent territories of the
four extraregional nations (France, Netherlands, United Kingdom, and
United States) in the Latin American/Caribbean region into three subregions:
Caribbean, Central America/Mexico, and South America. (See figure 2–1 and
table 2–1.) As a whole, this region accounts for about 15 percent of the
earth's land area, about 8 percent of the world's population, and about 6
percent of its gross national product. With respect to its economic develop-

Figure 2–1. The ICAO Latin America/Caribbean Region

Table 2–1
Countries in the ICAO Latin America/Caribbean Region

Caribbean	South America	Central America and Mexico
Contracting States	*Contracting States*	*Contracting States*
Antigua and Barbuda	Argentina	Costa Rica
Bahamas	Bolivia	El Salvador
Barbados	Brazil	Guatemala
Cuba	Chile	Honduras
Dominican Republic	Colombia	Mexico
Grenada	Ecuador	Nicaragua
Haiti	Guyana	Panama
Jamaica	Paraguay	
Saint Lucia	Peru	*Noncontracting State*
Trinidad and Tobago	Suriname	Belize
	Uruguay	
Noncontracting States	Venezuela	
Dominica		
Saint Vincent and the Grenadines		

Source: International Civil Aviation Organization (ICAO), *International Air Passenger and Freight Transport: Latin America and the Caribbean* (Montreal: ICAO, May 1983), 125.

ment, the region is positioned between the industrialized nations and the developing nations. Brazil and Mexico can be classified as the region's newly industrialized countries. With about one-third of the region's total population and a land area that exceeds that of the continental United States, Brazil is the largest country in the region. Brazil also boasts the world's ninth largest economy.

Demographically, as compared to other developing regions, a larger proportion of the region's population lives in urban areas. In South America, for example, two-thirds of the population are urban dwellers, a rate comparable to that of industrially developed regions. Even for the Caribbean subregion, where only about 50 percent of the population lives in urban areas, the rate is higher than that in other developing regions, in which urban dwellers account for less than one-third of the total population.[1] However, although this higher degree of urbanization is a favorable attribute in terms of the demand for air transportation services, a lower percentage of the population is economically active, which is a negative attribute.[2]

The region's economy experienced healthy growth during the 1960s and the 1970s. Since the beginning of the 1980s, however, a deterioration in economic growth, a diversion of resources needed to service unwieldy levels of foreign borrowing (estimated to be $400 billion at the end of 1986), and extremely high rates of inflation have significantly influenced the economic and social development of the region. These economic problems, combined with the policy mandates imposed by institutions such as the International Monetary Fund (IMF), have led many governments in the region to take drastic adjustment measures (in economic and fiscal policies), which in turn have reduced living standards and increased social tensions and political instability.

The Caribbean encompasses about two dozen islands, with a total population in excess of 30 million. The three largest nations in population are Cuba, the Dominican Republic, and Haiti. In 1984, the top three nations in terms of total GNP were the Dominican Republic ($7.2 billion in 1982 dollars), Jamaica ($3.8 billion), and Trinidad and Tobago ($3.1 billion). In terms of GNP per capita, the top three nations were the Bahamas ($6,700 in 1982 dollars), Barbados ($2,900), and Trinidad and Tobago ($2,700).[3] Not only are the Caribbean economies extremely small, but they are also highly vulnerable to external forces, such as (1) the economies of North America and Europe; (2) foreign-exchange rate movements; and (3) world prices for commodities exported from this subregion. In short, the Caribbean economies depend on foreign capital, markets, and technologies. Tourist travel is closely tied to the North American economy, to exchange rates, and to foreigners' perceptions of political turmoil and social problems (as exemplified by the experiences of Jamaica and Haiti).

There is widespread concern that severe belt-tightening among many Caribbean nations as a solution to their debt crises could become unbearable, thereby instigating social and political unrest and debtor cartels. Riots have already been observed in the Dominican Republic, Jamaica, and Haiti. It is ironic that although past integration attempts have not been very successful, the subregion's debt crisis may force greater collusion.

The situation in Central America, a subregion that faces many of the same economic and financial problems as the Caribbean islands, is more politically oriented. This area, which joins two continents and separates two oceans, has been plagued by the meddling of foreign powers that are interested in the subregion's geographic significance. The political situation and the resulting instability have been partly responsible for the retarded development of the air transport industry in this subregion. In terms of 1984 GNP, the three largest Central American nations are Guatemala (over $9 billion), Panama (over $4 billion), and El Salvador (almost $4 billion). In terms of GNP per capita, Panama dominates the subregion with a GNP per capita of more than $2,000 in 1984. Guatemala, Costa Rica, and Belize all had a GNP per capital of slightly more than $1,000 in 1984.

The economic and financial situation in South America is no different from that in the other two subregions. The top four economies in the South American subregion in 1984 were Brazil ($213 billion in 1982 dollars), Argentina ($58 billion), Venezuela ($39 billion), and Colombia ($30 billion). Their incomes per capital in 1984 were $1,625, $1,929, $2,340, and $1,045, respectively.[4] During the first half of this decade, the subregion's economy performed poorly. Brazil, with more than $100 billion in debt, is the largest debtor in the Third World. Inflation is one of Brazil's most serious chronic problems—over 200 percent in 1983 and again in 1984. Even though Brazil is generating sufficient funds to make payments on its external debt, the nation has not been able to contain inflation. In 1983, Argentina was carrying a $40 billion debt, inflation was running at an annual rate of about 500 percent, and investment had been declining for a number of years. During the first half of this decade, Venezuela's economy experienced negative or minute growth. Colombia has experienced an increase in foreign debt, unemployment, and public expenditure and a deterioration in the balance of payments.

In these four countries, as well as others in the subregion, austerity measures implemented to conform to the IMF requirements have had a negative impact on their economies in the short term and have led to—or in some cases simply accentuated—social tensions. In Brazil, for example, the social problem is quite serious, judging from the enormous gap between the rich and the poor. It is reported that during 1983–84, less than 8 percent of the population consumed 62 percent of the total consumption. At the other end of the spectrum, 9 percent of the population consumed less than one-twelfth of one percent of the total consumption.[5] Such a lopsided distribution of consumption not only leads to social tension but also limits the degree to which air transportation usage penetrates the total population.

Despite their current economic, financial, and social problems, selected countries in South America—especially Brazil and to a lesser extent Argentina—have tremendous potential for substantial economic development. Brazil, for example, has the geographic size, the population, and the economic base to become a world-class economy. It has become less dependent on foreign energy by increasing production and utilization of alcohol fuel, and it has diversified its exports by reducing coffee's contribution to export earnings and increasing the contribution of manufactured goods. Within the manufacturing sector, four trends are worth noting. First, Brazil is now the fifth largest producer and exporter of arms, the sales of which now account for 10 percent of all exports.[6] Second, although the proportion of trade with the United States decreased in the 1970s, it began to increase in the early 1980s. Third, Brazil is now manufacturing competitive, commuter-sized airplanes, which have gained considerable market acceptance in the United States. The Brazilian aircraft manufacturing potential is approaching the point where it could become a significant partner in jet transport development. Fourth, Brazil is beginning to develop a significantly large auto industry. Within the context of these developments, Brazil has the potential for emerging as one of the top economies in the world and, in turn, one of the top air transportation markets.

The Air Transportation System

The share of total worldwide traffic captured by the airlines registered in the Latin America/Caribbean region remained virtually the same between 1976 and 1985—just under 5 percent. However, there has been a significant shift in the international and domestic shares of the total traffic. During this ten-year period, the share of international traffic declined from 6.4 to 5.7 percent, while the share of domestic traffic increased from 3.5 to 4.1 percent.[7] The increase in the share of domestic traffic reflects national policies aimed at developing intranational air transportation markets, particularly in Mexico, Brazil, Argentina, and the Dominican Republic. In some cases, the objective is to develop new tourist destinations; in other cases, it is to facilitate the movement of passengers on business travel in domestic markets.

Scheduled air transportation services are provided by more than fifty airlines based in the region. Tables 2–2 through 2–4 provide traffic data on thirty-two airlines in the three subregions that reported such data to either IATA or ICAO in 1985. Nonscheduled services are provided by about two dozen carriers, most of which transport freight only. Finally, commuter carriers and air-taxi operators play a more important role in the Caribbean subregion than in other parts of the world because of the dispersion and isolation of many islands in this subregion.

The largest of the region's airlines are based in South America. Varig, the privately owned international airline of Brazil, is clearly the largest airline in this subregion. Varig's international service is well diversified. In 1985, passenger travel between Brazil and other countries in South America accounted for 37 percent of the total international travel; between Brazil and Europe, 32 percent; between Brazil and North America, 25 percent; and between Brazil and Africa, Asia, and Central America, 6 percent.[8] Varig's size, measured in revenue passenger miles, is comparable to Piedmont in the United States, South African Airways, or Thai International. Because of its size and importance, Varig has been able to upgrade its fleet, which now includes the B-747-300s, and is now offering good service at reasonable prices.

Brazil also has three airlines with significant domestic operations: VASP, TRANSBRASIL, and Cruzeiro. These four Brazilian airlines combined account for about 50 percent of the total output of the eighteen South American airlines listed in table 2–2 and about 30 percent of the activity of all thirty-two airlines in the region listed in tables 2–2 through 2–4. Worldwide, Brazil ranked eleventh in scheduled services provided by its airlines (measured in total ton-kilometers). Other relatively large airlines in South America are

Table 2–2
The Top Eighteen Airlines Based in South America, 1985

	Scheduled Services						
	Passengers (000)			Passenger-Kilometers (millions)			
Airline	Int'l	Dom.	Total	Int'l	Dom.	Total	Employees
Varig (Brazil)	1,070	3,683	4,753	7,072	3,000	10,072	19,383
Aerolineas Argentina	525	1,502	2,027	2,187	1,523	3,710	NA
VASP (Brazil)	—	3,536	3,536	—	3,391	3,391	8,275
AVIANCA (Colombia)	567	3,185	3,752	1,927	1,451	3,378	5,729
TRANSBRAZIL	—	2,172	2,172	—	2,577	2,577	5,238
Cruzeiro (Brazil)	227	2,109	2,336	298	1,957	2,255	3,513
VIASA (Venezuela)	535	—	535	2,117	—	2,117	2,787
Avensa (Venezuela)	—	2,312	2,312	—	1,439	1,439	NA
LanChile	210	177	387	959	321	1,280	NA
AeroPeru	184	723	906	552	441	993	1,681
Austral (Argentina)	—	1,208	1,208	—	967	967	7,792
LAB (Bolivia)	271	1,072	1,343	513	381	894	1,564
LAV (Venezuela)	60	1,960	2,020	21	792	813	2,066[a]
Ecuatoriana	206	—	206	754	—	754	988
Faucett (Peru)	40	638	678	152	454	607	1,290[a]
SAM (Colombia)	49	826	875	32	530	552	474
Ladeco (Chile)	59	311	370	191	315	506	486
Pluna (Uruguay)	245	—	245	371	—	371	828

Sources: International Air Transport Association (IATA), *World Air Transport Statistics* (Geneva: IATA, June 1986); and International Civil Aviation Organization (ICAO), *Civil Aviation Statistics of the World* (Montreal: ICAO, August 1986).
[a]1984 data.

Aerolineas, Argentina and AVIANCA, the international airline of Colombia. Both provide scheduled service within the region as well as to North America and Europe. Aerolineas Argentina also serves New Zealand.

Most of the scheduled service to, from, and within Central America is provided by the airlines listed in table 2–3. In general, these airlines are relatively small. For example, LACSA, the airline of Costa Rica, is about the size of Aloha or Hawaiian in the United States, Air Jugoslavia in Europe, or Air Zimbabwe in Africa. Some of the Central American carriers provide a significant proportion of their service to U.S. destinations. For example, TACA, the airline based in El Salvador, provides scheduled service to twelve international destinations, five of which are in the United States (Miami, New Orleans, Houston, Los Angeles, and San Francisco). In contrast, Air Panama

Table 2–3
**Scheduled Services of the Top Nine Airlines Based in Central America/
Mexico, 1985**

Airline	Passengers (000)			Passenger-Kilometers (millions)		
	Int'l	Dom.	Total	Int'l	Dom.	Total
Mexicana	2,285	6,367	8,652	5,012	4,394	9,606
Aeromexico	1,103	5,519	6,622	2,787	5,510	8,297
LACSA (Costa Rica)	282	—	282	557	—	557
TACA (El Salvador)	300	—	300	442	—	442
Dominicana	524	—	524	435	—	435
Air Panama	236	—	236	418	—	418
Aviateca (Guatemala)	78	22	100	138	6	144
COPA (Panama)	154	—	154	116	—	116
Sahsa (Honduras)	92	74	166	90	12	102

Sources: International Air Transport Association (IATA), *World Air Transport Statistics* (Geneva: IATA, June 1986); and International Civil Aviation Organization (ICAO), *Civil Aviation Statistics of the World* (Montreal: ICAO, August 1986).

provides service to six international destinations, only one of which (Miami) is in the United States.

Four carriers dominate the scheduled service provided in the Caribbean subregion: BWIA (International Trinidad and Tobago Airways Corporation), Cubana, Air Jamaica, and LIAT. (LIAT, the multinational airline owned by ten governments, did not report its traffic data for 1985, so it is not listed in table 2–4.) BWIA International, formed through the merger of the old BWIA (British West Indian Airways) and Trinidad and Tobago Air Services, provides scheduled service to a number of islands in the subregion and to destinations in North America and Europe (London). Cubana serves a number of destinations in the region, Montreal in North America, half a dozen cities in eastern and western Europe, and Angola and Mozambique in Africa. Air Jamaica provides scheduled service to eight destinations in the United States, two in the Caribbean, and one in Canada. LIAT operates extensive interisland scheduled service from Antigua. Although LIAT did not report its traffic data to ICAO for 1985, its size can be inferred from the size of its fleet. In 1986, LIAT's fleet consisted of six BAe 748s, eight BN-2s, and five DHC-6s. The airline also had five DHC-8s on order.[9]

The Regulatory Environment

The governments in this region stress "national interest" and therefore the "public service" nature of air transport. In general, the consensus is that reg-

Table 2–4
Scheduled Services of the Top Five Airlines Based in the Caribbean, 1985

	Passengers (000)			Passenger-Kilometers (millions)		
Airline[a]	Int'l	Dom.	Total	Int'l	Dom.	Total
BWIA (Trinidad/Tobago)	806	493	1,299	2,016	41	2,057
Cubana	226	669	895	1,459	342	1,801
Air Jamaica	832	16	848	1,478	2	1,480
Barbados Caribbean	32	—	32	214	—	214
Bahamasair	396	310	706	90	35	125[b]

Sources: International Air Transport Association (IATA), *World Air Transport Statistics* (Geneva: IATA, June 1986); and International Civil Aviation Organization (ICAO), *Civil Aviation Statistics of the World* (Montreal: ICAO, August 1986).
[a]Excludes LIAT, which did not report to either IATA or ICAO.
[b]1984 data.

ulation of the airline industry cannot be left to the forces of the marketplace to ensure a proper harmonization of supply and demand. Therefore, aeronautical authorities regulate capacity (using the predetermination approach), with the goal of providing equal opportunity (benefits) for airlines of each country on the basis of reciprocity. Although most markets tend to be served using third- and fourth-freedom rights, a number of carriers from North America and Europe do hold fifth-freedom rights in this region. In some cases, the fifth-freedom rights are exchanged for direct or indirect compensation. Until recently, governments had preferred that a single carrier provide international scheduled service. However, pooling arrangements have been accepted, particularly with European airlines. Regulations pertaining to nonscheduled service have been liberal in the Caribbean subregion but fairly tight in the South American subregion.

Although the foregoing regulatory philosophy is generally accepted in the region as a whole, there are some variations among subregions and within individual subregions. The regulatory approach within the Central American and Caribbean subregions can be characterized as ad hoc, particularly in the Caribbean. In these subregions, an individual country's attitude toward regulation is primarily a function of its economic situation and its desire to develop tourism. In South America, Chile was one of the first countries to embrace the philosophy that capacity should be regulated by the marketplace. More recently, a number of nations in the region—such as Panama, Venezuela, and Ecuador—have shown some interest in multiple designation for international operations.

Recent changes in the U.S. regulatory environment, coupled with the inability of a number of airlines in the region to modernize their fleets and the continuing diversion of tourism, could bring about changes in this region's regulatory attitude, particularly in the Caribbean. For example, although U.S. carriers have always been a significant force in the Caribbean marketplace, their operations are beginning to increase in the Caribben subregion, as evidenced by American Airlines' proposed establishment of a hub-and-spoke system in San Juan. Although the degree to which an effective hub-and-spoke system can be developed will depend on whether operating permits can be obtained from the governments of the islands, the smaller islands that do not have their own airlines (and the islands that do have their own airlines but do not have the resources to modernize their fleets) are likely to work with the U.S. airlines to fulfill their own interests. It is worth noting that in other regions of the world, the degree to which U.S. airlines could develop foreign-based hub-and-spoke systems has been limited by government route authority. Therefore, the Caribbean's economic reliance on U.S. tourist traffic will likely help the U.S.-based airlines get the traffic rights they seek.

Markets

Although true origin–destination passenger traffic statistics for this region are not readily available, a number of sources provide fragmented data that, when combined, provide an overview of the passenger markets in the region. Table 2–5 shows the relative size of thirteen passenger markets grouped by region pairs. Total traffic (scheduled plus charter in both directions) to, from, and within this region represents less than 12 percent of the world's total international traffic. By far the largest component of this region's traffic (about 10 million passengers) is between North America and Middle America (Central America/Mexico and Caribbean/Western Atlantic). South America accounts for 2.6 million passengers to and from North America, 2 million passengers within the subregion, and 1.8 million passengers to and from Europe.

In terms of tourism, of the 333 million tourist arrivals throughout the world in 1985, 20 million (6.1 percent) were visitors to the Latin America/Caribbean region. Of this 20 million, 12 million persons visited Central America/Mexico and South America and 8 million visited the Caribbean islands. Mexico accounted for more than a third of the visitors to Central America/Mexico and South America. Three other countries in these two subregions—Brazil, Argentina, and Uruguay—reported more than 1 million tourists each. Of the 8 million visitors to the Caribbean islands, Puerto Rico and the Bahamas alone accommodated almost 3 million. Other significant destinations (more than 300,000 visitors) included Jamaica, the Dominican Republic, the U.S. Virgin Islands, St. Maarten, and Bermuda.[10]

The majority of passengers traveling between North America and Middle America are traveling between the United States and the Caribbean islands.

Table 2–5
IATA International On-Flight Origin and Destination Traffic Statistics for Middle and South America, 1985

Region Pair	Passengers (000), (Both Directions)	Percentage of World Total
North America–Middle America	9,739	6.0
North America–South America	2,622	1.6
Middle America–South America	608	0.4
Middle America–Europe	1,130	0.7
Middle America–Africa	6	—
Middle America–Far East	17	—
Within Middle America	938	0.6
South America–Middle East	11	—
South America–Europe	1,830	1.1
South America–Africa	83	0.1
South America–Far East	51	—
South America–Southwest Pacific	29	—
Within South America	2,050	1.3
Subtotal	19,114	11.8
World total	162,418	

Source: International Air Transport Association (IATA), *World Air Transport Statistics, 1985* (Geneva: IATA, June 1986), 30.

In 1985, 4.8 million passengers arrived in the United States from the Caribbean (one-way traffic) using scheduled and charter flights. In 1985, the top three Caribbean destinations were the Bahamas, Jamaica, and the Dominican Republic (see table 2–6). Charter traffic accounted for about 15 percent of the total traffic between the United States and the Caribbean. Total scheduled traffic was three-fourths U.S. citizens and one-fourth foreigners. Two-thirds of the scheduled traffic moved on U.S. carriers and one-third on foreign-flag carriers such as Air Jamaica, Bahamasair, and BWIA (each of which serves six destinations in the United States).

Despite changes in U.S. tax laws that curtailed tax credits for business meetings in the Bahamas and other popular tourist spots—and, more recently, despite the drug scandals—the Bahamas is still the number one tourist destination in the Caribbean from the United States. In 1986, 3.7 million passengers traveled between the United States and the Bahamas, the fourth largest destination for U.S. travelers, after the United Kingdom, Mexico, and Japan. Although tourism is expected to continue to play an important role in the economy of the Bahamas, prices of ground services (such as hotels and meals) are beginning to divert tourists to less expensive islands (such as the

Table 2–6
Passenger Travel between the United States and the Latin America/Caribbean Region (Arrivals Only), 1985

| | Scheduled Flights | | | | |
| Country | U.S. Flag | | Foreign Flag | | |
	Aliens	Citizens	Aliens	Citizens	Total (%)
Central America/Mexico	506,823	837,550	623,568	1,318,450	3,286,391 (96)
Belize	2,811	1,354	14,341	22,013	40,519 (99)
Costa Rica	20,109	32,789	44,588	40,785	138,271 (99)
El Salvador	8,457	1,951	54,244	40,483	105,135 (97)
Guatemala	19,637	18,560	41,887	26,997	107,081 (100)
Honduras	15,640	4,972	39,508	39,783	99,903 (98)
Mexico	398,748	713,721	383,154	1,101,532	2,597,155 (95)
Nicaragua	140	40	7,832	6,639	14,651 (98)
Panama Canal Zone (U.S.)	0	0	0	0	0 (0)
Panama Republic	41,281	64,163	36,133	37,938	179,515 (100)
San Andres Island	0	0	1,881	2,280	4,161 (100)
Caribbean	484,749	2,086,314	531,520	990,260	4,092,843 (86)
Anguilla Island	74	175	115	73	437 (23)
Antigua	13,490	132,760	14,269	21,991	182,510 (98)
Bahama Islands	175,831	635,723	135,735	179,471	1,126,760 (75)
Barbados	33,585	120,888	19,050	32,669	206,192 (95)
Bermuda	25,639	377,737	2,526	8,702	414,604 (95)
Cuba	26	10	0	0	36 (0)
Dominica	12	52	52	156	272 (23)
Dominican Republic	55,956	218,596	87,767	221,857	584,176 (96)
Grand Cayman	10,000	40,730	33,625	79,888	164,243 (95)
Grenada	0	0	707	1,984	2,691 (99)
Guadeloupe	4,069	14,263	5,693	6,592	30,617 (87)
Haiti	54,927	82,559	26,963	22,149	186,598 (97)
Jamaica	40,770	181,513	112,682	286,475	621,440 (88)
Martinique	5,490	30,273	1,297	4,778	41,838 (90)
Montserrat I	2	7	0	0	9 (26)
Neth. Antilles	34,505	188,781	31,812	43,993	299,091 (73)
Nevis	83	439	119	94	735 (89)
Providencial Islands	2,130	2,531	231	646	5,538 (34)
St Barthelmy	630	2,611	0	0	3,241 (97)
St Kitts	1,917	4,546	5,267	6,875	18,605 (97)
St Lucia	3,339	9,900	3,288	7,147	23,674 (95)
St Vincent	0	0	0	0	0 (0)
Trinidad/Tobago	18,371	23,885	38,363	36,369	116,988 (99)

| | *Chartered Flights* | | | | |
| U.S. Flag | | Foreign Flag | | | Grand Total |
Aliens	*Citizens*	*Aliens*	*Citizens*	*Total (%)*	*Grand Total*
4,777	101,673	2,137	23,446	132,033 (4)	3,418,424
122	153	19	91	385 (1)	40,904
392	1,096	180	250	1,918 (1)	140,189
878	1,125	698	1,080	3,781 (3)	108,916
3	120	91	79	293 (0)	107,374
1,241	372	32	120	1,765 (2)	101,668
1,909	98,423	804	21,723	122,859 (5)	2,720,014
192	53	6	0	251 (2)	14,902
3	195	0	0	198 (100)	198
37	136	307	103	583 (0)	180,098
0	0	0	0	0 (0)	4,161
33,304	591,319	16,021	39,853	680,497 (14)	4,773,340
477	765	67	141	1,450 (77)	1,887
48	2,675	94	375	3,192 (2)	185,702
15,879	345,726	1,470	12,696	375,771 (25)	1,502,531
678	8,548	559	229	10,014 (5)	216,206
71	17,456	18	2,047	19,592 (5)	434,196
6,455	8,167	18	8	14,648 (100)	14,684
263	484	60	93	900 (77)	1,172
1,367	12,875	827	6,976	22,045 (4)	606,221
17	1,260	2,690	5,118	9,085 (5)	173,328
6	22	0	0	28 (1)	2,719
141	3,986	273	229	4,629 (13)	35,246
400	3,466	935	531	5,332 (3)	191,930
2,051	74,563	6,159	3,205	85,978 (12)	707,418
85	4,494	12	0	4,591 (10)	46,429
9	12	0	4	25 (74)	34
3,542	95,562	1,727	7,355	108,186 (27)	407,277
10	58	0	21	89 (11)	824
690	9,543	63	281	10,577 (66)	16,115
15	85	8	4	112 (3)	3,353
60	428	13	140	641 (3)	19,246
199	133	691	152	1,175 (5)	24,849
17	0	1	0	18 (100)	18
680	408	234	66	1,388 (1)	118,376

Table 2–6 continued

| | Scheduled Flights | | | | |
| Country | U.S. Flag | | Foreign Flag | | |
	Aliens	Citizens	Aliens	Citizens	Total (%)
Turks/Caicos	1,227	978	3,191	4,165	9,561 (98
Virgin Islands (U.K.)	2,676	17,357	8,768	24,186	52,987 (98
South America	236,344	204,526	441,376	333,986	1,216,232 (97
Argentina	14,177	12,090	34,461	22,517	83,245 (100
Bolivia	3,199	2,728	15,455	7,947	29,329 (100
Brazil	48,289	57,060	129,462	91,076	325,887 (93
Chile	11,993	10,583	22,103	14,577	59,256 (99
Colombia	59,118	47,781	90,175	79,568	276,642 (99
Ecuador	24,806	26,850	30,417	36,988	119,061 (99
Fr. Guiana	0	0	0	0	0 (0
Guyana	59	429	6,625	12,712	19,825 (100
Paraguay	900	939	11,465	7,544	20,848 (100
Peru	0	0	13,957	13,444	27,401 (100
Surinam	0	0	6,837	1,538	8,375 (100
Uruguay	154	293	0	0	447 (100
Venezuela	73,649	45,773	80,419	46,075	245,916 (99

Source: U.S. Department of Transportation, *U.S. International Air Travel Statistics* (Cambridge, Mass.: U.S. DOT, May 1986), 1–2.

Dominican Republic), especially those with a favorable exchange rate. Recently, it has also been observed that the spending per tourist in the Bahamas has been declining. To offset the impact of this trend, the government is promoting low-cost packages for Bahamians to do more traveling at home.[11]

In Jamaica, the second most popular tourist destination in the Caribbean from the United States, the benefit of recent currency devaluations has been partly offset by high inflation and political unrest. The tourism industry is Jamaica's second largest foreign-exchange earner (behind bauxite), but future prospects for the demand for air travel depend very heavily on the performance of the economy, political stability, and the cost of tourist services. Jamaica can ill afford to lose tourist revenues, because its debt burden (measured as a percentage of GNP) was the highest in the region.[12]

Although the Dominican Republic has also been experiencing severe economic and financial problems (high unemployment, mounting foreign debt, and deteriorating trade imbalances), the nation has been the beneficiary of tourist diversions from other islands that have priced themselves out of the marketplace. The Dominican Republic is now the third largest tourist desti-

| | | Chartered Flights | | | |
| U.S. Flag | | Foreign Flag | | | Grand Total |
Aliens	Citizens	Aliens	Citizens	Total (%)	
41	98	41	19	199 (2)	9,760
103	505	61	163	832 (2)	53,819
2,343	17,017	10,539	2,037	31,936 (3)	1,248,168
2	3	147	240	392 (0)	83,637
0	0	62	23	85 (0)	29,414
2,053	15,916	7,524	486	25,979 (7)	351,866
0	0	149	377	526 (1)	59,782
14	263	1,881	156	2,314 (1)	278,956
185	215	256	22	678 (1)	119,739
9	133	0	5	147 (100)	147
16	7	0	0	23 (0)	19,848
0	0	2	0	2 (0)	20,850
0	0	0	0	0 (0)	27,401
0	0	24	0	24 (0)	8,399
0	0	0	0	0 (0)	447
64	480	494	728	1,766 (1)	247,682

nation in the Caribbean from the United States. However, economic malaise, government austerity measures, and the guidelines set by the IMF (as requirements for the continuation of extended credit arrangements) have led to uprisings by the urban poor and protests by unions and students. It is estimated that nearly 85 percent of the export income is needed to pay for the foreign debt alone, leaving very few resources for the social programs.[13] The government has been attempting to diversify its economy by reducing its dependence on sugar and expanding the tourist business—policies that not only should improve economic conditions but also should enhance political stability.

In Cuba, which has been politically isolated from the West for the past three decades, the government has recently begun to promote tourism, a source of critically needed foreign currency. It should be recalled that Cuba was once a strong tourist destination in the Caribbean. In 1957, 272,000 foreigners visited Cuba—87 percent from the United States.[14] After the revolution, tourist traffic dwindled, but it has been increasing steadily since 1975. It is estimated that 168,000 foreigners visited Cuba in 1985—51,000 from Europe, 40,000 from Canada, 27,000 from the Socialist countries, 27,000 from Latin America, 15,000 from Asia and Africa, and 8,000 from other countries.[15] The most significant trend is the influx of Canadian tourists. Continued relaxation of the visiting restrictions, coupled with on-going development of the tourist infrastructure and aggressive promotion of diverse tourist attractions, could help Cuba develop into a significant tourist hub. Tourism, in turn, could diversify Cuba's economy, which in the past has been dependent on sugar on one hand and the Cuban–Soviet grants on the other.

The total passenger market between the United States and Central America (including Mexico) is about 70 percent of the market between the United States and the Caribbean. Mexico represents about 80 percent of the total market and Central America about 20 percent. The two largest passenger markets from the United States to the rest of Central America are Panama and Costa Rica (see table 2–6). Less than 4 percent of the total traffic moved on charter flights. Two-thirds of the scheduled traffic passengers were U.S. citizens. The total scheduled market in 1985 was shared 40 percent by U.S.-flag carriers and 60 percent by foreign-flag carriers. During 1986, 377,000 passengers traveled between the United States and Panama, compared to almost 4 million to the Bahamas. Table 2–7 shows the relative importance of travel between the United States and the various nations in the Latin America/Caribbean region in 1986.

In 1985, the total passenger market between the United States and South America was less than 40 percent of the Central America/Mexico market and less than 30 percent of the Caribbean market. The three largest markets between the United States and South America are Brazil, Colombia, and Venezuela. (Tables 2–6 and 2–7 show the size of these markets in 1985 and 1986.) Between South America and Europe, the three largest scheduled passenger markets are between Rio de Janeiro and Madrid, Paris, and Frankfurt. Within South America, the three largest markets are between Buenos Aires and Montevideo, Rio de Janeiro, and Santiago. Obviously, Brazil (Varig) is the preeminent air travel generator in South America. The scheduled airline network to, from, and within South America is quite extensive. Table 2–8 lists the international destinations to which nonstop scheduled service was available at the beginning of 1987 from the top ten cities in South America. More than twenty-five international destinations receive scheduled service from Caracas and Rio de Janeiro.

Fares

A comparison of the normal economy fares between North America and Central America/Caribbean during September 1985 shows that the average fares were lower than the world average for long-haul trips (over 2,000 km) and higher than the world average for distances less than 1,000 km. (See table 2–9.) Markets in this sample do not include Alaska, Hawaii, or Mexico. Out of a sample of 282 markets, 140 (about 50 percent) had stage lengths greater than 2,000 km. For markets within Central America and the Caribbean, nor-

Table 2–7
Passenger Travel between the United States and the Latin
America/Caribbean Region, 1986

Country	Total Passengers (000)	% U.S. Citizen	Scheduled Service U.S. Flag	Scheduled Service Foreign Flag	Charter as % of Total
Bahamas	3,692	77	2,198	873	17
Jamaica	1,624	78	545	876	12
Dominican Republic	1,301	80	762	511	2
Neth. Antilles	870	83	606	133	15
Brazil	828	43	374	410	5
Colombia	549	49	212	335	0
Venezuela	508	44	279	226	0
Barbados	428	81	302	103	5
Panama Republic	377	61	262	113	0
Grand Cayman	371	76	98	252	6
Haiti	340	59	277	60	1
Guatemala	308	47	138	167	1
Costa Rica	297	58	116	179	1
Antigua	260	80	149	100	4
Ecuador	244	53	102	141	0
Honduras	215	51	43	172	0
El Salvador	197	49	24	172	1
Trinidad/Tobago	177	52	65	109	2
Chile	107	44	47	58	1
Virgin Islands (U.K.)	107	84	29	77	1

Source: Data provided by the U.S. Department of Transportation.

mal economy fares tended to be higher than the world average for distances under 1,000 km and lower than the world average for distances higher than 1,000 km. However, within the Caribbean, fares to northern Caribbean islands were reasonably competitive, whereas southern Caribbean fares tended to be cost-based.

For markets within South America, normal fares were considerably below the world average for all distances.[16] Table 2–10 shows the relationship between average fares and normal economy fares in the local South America subregion and the world. Throughout the entire twelve-year period shown, the average local fares for travel within South America have been higher—occasionally much higher—than the world average. Since 1981, the ratio of the average fare to the normal economy fare in this subregion has begun to approach the world average. One reason for this change is an increase in charter operations, particularly to Brazil.

Table 2–8
Nonstop Service between City Pairs, Latin America/Caribbean Region

Rio de Janeiro	Caracas	Buenos Aires	Bogota	Sao Paulo	Lima	Santiago	Quito	Guayaquil	La Paz
Abidjan	Amsterdam	Asuncion	Arica	Asuncion	Asuncion	Asuncion	Bogota	Bogota	Arica
Amsterdam	Aruba	Auckland	Caracas	Buenos Aires	Bogota	Bogota	Cayenne	Buenos Aires	Asuncion
Asuncion	Barbados	Caracas	Guayaquil	Frankfurt	Buenos Aires	Buenos Aires	Lima	Curacao	Cali
Bogota	Bogota	Guayaquil	Lima	Iguazu	Caracas	Caracas	Mexico City	Jujuy	Jujuy
Buenos Aires	Bonaire	Havana	Manaus	Miami	Guayaquil	Easter Is.	Miami	Lima	Lima
Caracas	Buenos Aires	Iguassu Falls	Mexico City	Montevideo	Havana	Guayaquil	Panama City	Mexico City	Santiago
Casablanca	Curacao	Las Palmas	Miami	Santa Cruz	La Paz	La Paz	San Jose	Miami	
Frankfurt	Fort-de-France	Lima	Panama City	Santiago	Los Angeles	Lima	San Juan	New York	
Geneva	Frankfurt	Madrid	Quito		Mexico City	Los Angeles		Panama City	
Guayaquil	Greneda	Miami	Rio de Janeiro		Montego Bay	Mendoza		Santiago	
Lima	Lima	Montevideo	San Juan		New York	Miami		San Paulo	
Lisbon	Lisbon	New York	Santiago		Quito	Montevideo			
London	Madrid	Porto Alegre			Rio de Janeiro	Panama City			
Los Angeles	Manaus	Rio de Janeiro			San Jose	Porto Alegre			

		Santa Cruz	Sao Paulo
		Santiago	
		Sao Paulo	
		Toronto	

Luanda	Miami	Santa Cruz
Madrid	Milan	Santiago
Miami	New York	Sao Paulo
Milan	Panama City	
Montevideo	Paris	
New York	Port of Spain	
Panama City	Porto	
Paris	Rio de Janeiro	
Porto	St. Lucia	
Rome	San Juan	
Toronto	Santiago	
Zurich	Santo Domingo	
	Tenerife	
	Zurich	

Source: Official Airlines Guides (OAG), *Official Airline Guide: Worldwide Edition* (Oak Brook, Ill.: OAG, January 1987).

Table 2–9
Comparison of Average Normal Economy Fares per Passenger-Kilometer in the Latin America/Caribbean Region, September 1985

Route Group	Cents/Passenger-Kilometer, by Distance (km)						
	250	*500*	*1,000*	*2,000*	*3,000*	*4,000*	*6,000*
Between North America and Central America/ Caribbean	32.2	23.8	17.6	13.0	—	9.6	—
Between and Within Central America and the Caribbean	32.0	24.4	18.7	14.3	12.2	—	—
Local South America	20.4	17.8	15.5	13.5	—	11.8	10.9
International Average— World	28.7	23.6	19.4	16.0	—	13.2	—

Source: International Civil Aviation Organization (ICAO), *Survey of International Air Transport Fares and Rates, September 1985* (Montreal: ICAO, June 1986).

Table 2–10
Average Revenue per Passenger-Kilometer as a Percentage of Average Normal Economy Fare per Passenger-Kilometer, South America and World

Year	Local South America	World
1973	81	54
1974	62	51
1975	80	58
1976	75	56
1977	79	63
1978	80	62
1979	84	60
1980	85	58
1981	91	58
1982	84	59
1983	77	53
1984	77[a]	69[a]

Source: Data provided by the International Civil Aviation Organization.

[a]In 1984, ICAO changed the definition of the normal economy fare. Between 1973 and 1983, the lowest level of economy fare was included in the analysis; in 1984, it was the highest level of normal economy fare.

In the past, a number of airlines based in this region had opted to stay out of the IATA traffic conference machinery. The presence of non-IATA members operating basically in the Central America and Caribbean subregions, coupled with a substantial amount of charter operations, maintained a semblance of competition in airline fares. Nonetheless, normal economy fares to and from South America have remained relatively high compared to the world average for comparable distances, partly because of such factors as the thinness of passenger markets, differences in operating costs, and the tightly controlled environment. Airlines generally have not discounted fares in their own countries—at least not in countries where fares have been based on dollars—but they have practiced discounting to varying degrees outside their own countries.

In the future, fares are likely to decline in this region because of a number of factors. First, two major airlines (Aeromexico and Mexicana) have decided to leave the IATA traffic coordinating group. Second, a number of U.S. airlines are expanding their operations in this region. Third, a number of airlines based in this region that have a significant proportion of their operations to the United States will be under pressure to maintain lower fares. Fourth, several nations (for example, the Dominican Republic) are attempting to increase the tourism component of their economies, and they will undoubtedly pressure their national carriers to keep fare increases to a minimum. Finally, the increase in charter activity will force a reduction in scheduled fares.

Financial Performance of the Carriers

As in other regions, this region's airlines have been examining alternative ways to reduce operating costs and increase revenues. On the cost side, table 2–11 shows the regional differences in estimated costs per passenger—kilometer by cost item for 1984. Compared to the world average, all subregions in Latin America and the Caribbean experienced high unit operating costs. Within local South America, passenger costs per passenger—kilometer were 10.9 cents, compared to 6.96 cents for the world average.[17] In addition, the airlines based in this region have been negatively affected by other factors, such as devaluation of their currencies and difficulty in meeting their debt-servicing requirements. The airlines that have been able to obtain concessions from their creditors are in a slightly better position to manage the coming challenges.

A number of the region's airlines are facing the possibility of not being able to utilize their older airplanes (such as B-707s and DC-8s) in the markets to the United States and Europe because of noise considerations. They cannot afford to buy modern equipment, and although options do exist to hush-kit the older airplanes, there are uncertainties with respect to their cost-effective-

Table 2–11
Estimated Passenger Costs per Passenger-Kilometer, by Cost Item, 1984

Route Groups	Total Operating Costs (sum columns 1–9)	Aircraft Operating Costs				Other Operating Costs				
		Costs Excluding Fuel and Oil[a] (1)	Fuel and Oil (2)	Landing and Associated Airport Charges (3)	En-Route Facility Charges (4)	Station Expenses (5)	Passenger Service (6)	Commission (7)	Ticketing, Sales, and Promotion (8)	General, Administrative, and Miscellaneous (9)
I. ALL										
U.S. cents	6.96	1.75	1.63	0.23	0.11	0.64	0.86	0.66	0.64	0.44
Percentage of total costs	100.0	25.1	23.4	3.3	1.6	9.2	12.4	9.5	9.2	6.3
II. International Route Groups (U.S. cents)										
1. North–Central America	7.9	2.1	1.8	0.2	0.0	1.1	0.9	0.6	0.6	0.6
2. Central America	9.8	2.3	2.4	0.4	0.1	1.3	0.6	0.9	1.0	0.8
3. North America	7.8	2.1	1.6	0.2	0.0	1.3	0.9	0.6	0.6	0.5
4. North–South America	8.0	2.3	2.0	0.2	0.1	0.7	0.8	0.8	0.7	0.4
5. South America	10.9	2.9	3.0	0.6	0.2	0.8	0.8	1.0	1.1	0.5

12.1	2.8	2.2	0.8	0.4	1.6	1.3	1.1	1.5	0.4
6. Europe									
–	–	–	–	–	–	–	–	–	–
7. Middle East									
10.4	2.6	3.1	0.5	0.1	0.9	0.7	0.8	0.7	0.8
8. Africa									
9.3	2.7	2.0	0.3	0.2	0.7	1.0	0.8	0.8	0.9
9. Europe–Middle East									
7.3	1.7	2.1	0.2	0.1	0.5	0.8	0.6	0.7	0.6
10. Europe–Africa									
5.5	1.2	1.3	0.1	0.1	0.5	0.8	0.5	0.5	0.5
11. North Atlantic									
6.2	1.5	1.8	0.2	0.1	0.4	0.7	0.4	0.6	0.5
12. Mid Atlantic									
7.9	2.1	2.1	0.2	0.1	0.7	0.8	0.7	0.8	0.4
13. South Atlantic									
6.9	2.0	1.4	0.3	0.1	0.6	0.8	0.8	0.6	0.3
14. Asia-Pacific									
6.0	1.5	1.5	0.2	0.1	0.4	0.8	0.6	0.5	0.4
15. Europe–Asia-Pacific									
5.3	1.3	1.4	0.1	0.0	0.3	0.8	0.7	0.4	0.3
16. North–Mid Pacific									
6.2	1.5	1.6	0.1	0.0	0.6	0.9	0.6	0.5	0.4
17. South Pacific									

Source: International Civil Aviation Organization (ICAO), *Regional Differences in Fares, Rates and Costs for International Air Transport, 1984* (Montreal: ICAO, July 1986), 11.

Note: "Passenger" costs have been derived for each route group, taking into account the contribution made by the revenue earned for the carriage of freight and mail toward covering total costs. Due to the margins of uncertainty in the estimates of individual cost items, the figures should be regarded as indicative only.

[a]This item includes flight operations expenses (cockpit crew salaries and expenses, rentals and insurance of flight equipment), aircraft maintenance and overhaul, and aircraft standing charges such as depreciation and interest charges.

ness. Some of the region's airlines are using equipment that is too big to serve their routes economically. However, because of national pride, these airlines are reluctant to buy smaller, more appropriate turboprops, even though such equipment would enable these carriers to increase frequency, thereby improving service and stimulating demand. Leasing cost-effective airplanes might be an option, but other considerations must be taken into account: (1) the Tax Reform Act of 1984, which virtually eliminated investment tax credits and the Accelerated Cost Recovery System (ACRS) with respect to U.S.-registered airplanes operating to and from the United States; and (2) the financially weak position of a number of airlines and governments in the region.

Future Prospects

The future of the airline industry in the Latin America/Caribbean region is tied very closely to the economic and financial conditions of the nations within the region. The governments, in turn, face major challenges, including managing the external debt effectively, stimulating foreign trade, increasing employment opportunities, and containing inflation. Although the governments in the region have been making remedial adjustments, some aspects of the solution to these problems depend on external developments, such as the international petroleum market, international commodity prices, and the conditions of the U.S. economy. Major uncertainties persist: Can sufficient structural reforms be implemented to contain inflation in the near term? Will international creditors exercise greater flexibility? What role will the IMF play in the region? Will the economic problems and the resulting internal discontent slow the pace of economic and social reform or lead to the establishment of military regimes in countries with civilian forms of government? Will countries in which political power changes hands from military to civilian rule experience a delay in the implementation of changes in the economic policies because of the greater amounts of time needed for debate and consultation?[18]

Despite present economic conditions, however, there is optimism. For example, the ailing sugar sectors could be revived by producing alcohol, which could then be used to substitute for petroleum imports.[19] In Central America, the strategy might be to place more emphasis on manufacturing activities in the tariff-free zone.[20] Foreign risk investments might be attracted if governments could implement policy changes, such as reducing limitations to the remittances of foreign business entities.

The economic and financial condition of the region relates directly to the most critical challenge facing the airline industry in this region—namely, the need to replace older airplanes that not only are inefficient but do not meet the noise standards for operations to the United States and Europe, two markets on which the region depends very heavily for passenger traffic. As two examples, consider the fleets of Ecuatoriana and LanChile. As of 1986, Ecuatoriana had six airplanes in its fleet: four B-707s were models introduced between 1966 and 1969; one B-720 was a 1961 model; and the remaining DC-10 was a 1972 model. Similarly, five of LanChile's eleven airplanes were B-707s of 1963 to 1968 vintage. Clearly, these airplanes will have to be replaced if they are to serve markets in the United States and Europe, but the airlines and their owner governments are already heavily indebted, and international lending authorities are imposing stricter controls.

There are five options for equipment upgrades, with varying degrees of viability: (1) to lease airplanes that are likely to be used; (2) to establish operating agreements with airlines that have modern airplanes and that are interested in serving markets in this region; (3) to consolidate operations with other airlines in the region; (4) to work with airplane manufacturers that are willing to assist with the financing to sell their airplanes; and (5) to reassign airplanes to markets within the region and to markets in Africa that are not noise-sensitive. Each option has advantages and disadvantages. For example, greater participation by the manufacturers in financing could mean that some airlines might select airplanes not so much according to the needs of the markets served but rather on the basis of the attractiveness of the financing package from a particular manufacturer.

The second challenge facing the airlines based in the Caribbean subregion is to control the diversion of tourism from high-cost destinations to low-cost destinations. The high-cost islands, such as the Bahamas and Antigua, could lose their tourist traffic to the lower-cost islands, such as the Dominican Republic, and to countries in Central America/Mexico, such as Costa Rica. Not only are these nations beginning to provide well-defined products that offer value for money, but they are beginning to develop their provincial areas as new tourist destinations. Examples include new tourist areas in Mexico and the Dominican Republic. Countries with favorable exchange rates, such as Mexico, provide added incentives for tourists. The airlines based in the region will undoubtedly be affected by the diversionary impact on tourism. For example, the increase in tourist travel has allowed Dominicana to offer B-747 service from Santa Domingo to New York.

The third challenge facing the airlines based in the Caribbean subregion is a strategy for dealing with the U.S. airlines' increased service to the Caribbean markets. Such U.S. carriers as Eastern and Pan American have always had a significant presence in the region. Now American Airlines has announced the development of a hub at San Juan. Assuming that most of the airlines based in the Caribbean cannot match either the efficiency of U.S. airlines or their traffic feed, the local airlines face the choice of competing head-on with the U.S. airlines or joining forces with them—for example, by becoming their feeders. Such a strategy would change the shape of the local airlines' fleets and networks. For example, a feeder airline might find it more appropriate to operate small modern turboprops (such as the Brasilia, the Dash-8 and the ATR-42) to San Juan rather than jets (such as B-737s and MD-80s) to Miami. Such a development would change not only the shape of the Caribbean-based airlines but also the stature of Miami as a gateway for Caribbean operations. A similar change could also take place in Central America, where Pan American once operated a reasonable size hub in Guatemala City.

The economic and financial conditions of the nations in the region, coupled with the developments in the three aforementioned areas, could have an enormous impact on the structure and performance of the airlines industry based in the Latin America/Caribbean region. For example, despite the nations' desires to maintain their own independent airlines, the smaller airlines based in the Caribbean subregion may be forced to cooperate more with the larger airlines from North America and Europe and, in turn, to change their networks and fleets to optimize the benefits for both partners. In Central America, the politically stable nations have the potential of increasing tourism in the long run, given their lower cost relative to other tourist destinations in the Caribbean. An increase in tourism, in turn, will increase the size of their airline operations and the contribution to their economies. The smaller countries in South America may be forced to combine some of their operations and offer joint services, partly to overcome their meager resources and partly to compete more effectively with the carriers from North America and Europe, on the one hand, and Brazil, on the other. Furthermore, as tourist destinations, the politically stable countries in South America have the real potential of becoming either alternative destinations to Europe or new destinations for frequent travelers who have already visited Europe.

Notes

1. International Civil Aviation Organization (ICAO), *International Air Passenger and Freight Transport: Latin America and the Caribbean* (Montreal: ICAO, May 1983), 3.

2. Ibid.

3. Jack W. Hopkins, ed., *Latin America and the Caribbean Contemporary Record,* Vol. IV (New York: Holmes and Meier, 1986).

4. Ibid., 987.

5. Thomas C. Bruneau and Anne-Marie Smith, "Brazil," in *Latin America and Caribbean Contemporary Record,* Vol. IV, ed. Jack W. Hopkins (New York: Holmes and Meier, 1986), 265–83.

6. Ibid., 278.

7. International Civil Aviation Organization (ICAO), *Bulletin* (Montreal: ICAO, June 1986), 25.

8. Rubel Thomas, "Factors Impacting Latin American Air Travel Demand," *Twelfth Annual FAA Aviation Forecast Conference Proceedings* (Washington, D.C.: FAA, February 1987), 90–101.

9. Gunter G. Endres, *World Airline Fleets* (London: Aviation Data Centre, 1986), 284.

10. World Tourism Organization, *Compendium of Tourism Statistics* (Madrid: WTO, 1986).

11. Hopkins, *Latin America and Caribbean*, 627.

12. Ibid., 748.

13. Ibid., 702.

14. The Economist Publications Limited, *International Tourism Report: Cuba*, National Report Number 116 (London: The Economist, May 1986), 69–79.

15. Ibid.

16. International Civil Aviation Organization (ICAO), *Survey of International Air Transport Fares and Rates, September 1985* (Montreal: ICAO, June 1986).

17. International Civil Aviation Organization (ICAO), *Regional Differences in Fares, Rates and Costs for International Air Transport* (Montreal: ICAO, July 1986), 11.

18. Robin Chapman, "Latin America and the Caribbean: Economic Problems," in *South America, Central America and the Caribbean, 1986* (London: Europa Publications, 1986), 9.

19. Scott B. MacDonald and F. Joseph Demetrius, "The Caribbean Debt Crisis," in *Latin America and Caribbean Contemporary Record*, Vol. IV, ed. Jack W. Hopkins (New York: Holmes and Meier, 1986), 87–94.

20. John Weeks, "The Central American Economies in 1984 and 1985," in *Latin America and Caribbean Contemporary Record*, Vol. IV, ed. Jack W. Hopkins (New York: Holmes and Meier, 1986), 106–14.

3
Europe

The economic successes of the United States and some Pacific Rim countries have inspired some governments around the globe to begin relaxing control of certain sectors of their economies, including the aviation industry. Although pressure to change the regulatory structure of air transportation services in Europe has been mounting for years, it has become far more critical since the middle of this decade. The trend toward free-market determination has gathered substantial momentum since the beginning of the international liberalization movement in the United States and the actions taken by some progressive nations in Europe.

Despite the growing pressure for regulatory reform, there remains an enormous disparity of opinion among the European governments regarding the benefits and the feasibility of airline deregulation. Almost all governments in Europe argue that the attributes of the European air transportation system—coupled with the wide variation in economic, social, and political philosophies among the European nations—preclude full-scale U.S.-style deregulation. Some European governments go further and argue against any regulatory reforms on the basis of the institutional differences between North America and Europe. At the other extreme, the independent actions of a few influential countries that do believe in the merits of regulatory reform are forcing other nations to make competitive changes. As a result, the existing system has become less tightly regulated and more competitive. Furthermore, the European Economic Community (EEC) continues to propose liberalization and even has threatened to take to the European Court of Justice those airlines that do not stop anticompetitive practices.

This chapter begins with a brief description of the regional economics and demographics, followed by an examination of the existing European air transportation system. An understanding of these fundamental characteristics will provide a perspective on the forces for and against the liberalization movement in Europe, the progress that has been made toward a liberal European air services regime, and the extent of the reforms that can be expected in the future. Based on these trends and the actions already taken by some airlines to reposition themselves in the new environment, the chapter also attempts to explain the most likely future developments in the European airline industry.

Regional Economic and Geographic Factors

Although there is no unique way of defining Europe, some geographers and historians believe that a broad definition should include the thirty-four countries west of the Russian Ural mountains. This group includes thirteen western European nations; Scandinavia; eight iron curtain nations; the island nations of Iceland, Malta, and Cyprus; and parts of the Soviet Union and Turkey. Also included are some extremely small nations—such as Andorra, Liechtenstein, Monaco, and San Marino—which combined encompass an area of less than 400 square miles and a population of about one-half million persons. More than fifty languages are spoken by the 700 million people living in this region. Including the approximately 200 million people living in the western part of the Soviet Union, Europe accounts for about 15 percent of the world's population and is the second most densely populated continent in the world.

Given the extreme diversity of the thirty-four countries in this group—and the fact that some of the countries play no role in the changing European airline industry—the definition of Europe will henceforth be confined to the twenty-two member nations of the European Civil Aviation Conference (ECAC), as shown in figure 3–1 and table 3–1. Even this is an area of great diversity with respect to the number of languages, number of frontiers, and population densities. For the purposes of this chapter, however, the ECAC nations are reasonably representative of trends in the European air transportation industry. Later in this chapter, the discussion will focus on an even smaller group of nations in western Europe, the European Economic Community (EEC). The twelve members of the EEC, which account for almost half of the total population of Europe, are also part of the twenty-two-nation ECAC. (These twelve western European nations are also listed in table 3–1.)

Among the twenty-two ECAC nations, West Germany, France, and Great Britain hold dominant positions (in that order) in terms of the size of their economies and the level of trade with other countries. Although each of these countries has exports and imports in excess of $100 billion, West Germany not only ranks first in trade value but has a value of exports far exceeding its value of imports. Moreover, West Germany is the major trading partner for two-thirds of the ECAC countries. Only three other ECAC countries export significantly more than they import (Norway, Sweden, and the Netherlands).

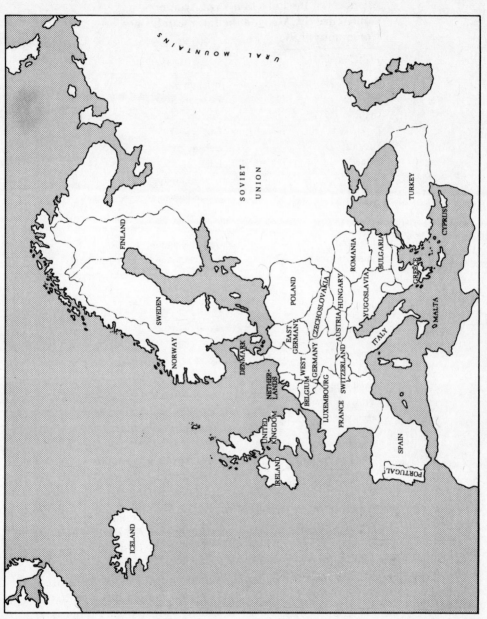

Figure 3–1. The ECAC Europe Region

Table 3–1
Members of the European Civil Aviation
Conference (ECAC) and the European Economic
Community (EEC)

ECAC Members	EEC Members
Austria	Belgium
Belgium	Denmark
Cyprus	France
Denmark	Greece
Finland	Ireland
France	Italy
Greece	Luxemburg
Iceland	Netherlands
Ireland	Portugal
Italy	Spain
Luxemburg	United Kingdom
Malta	West Germany
Netherlands	
Norway	
Portugal	
Spain	
Sweden	
Switzerland	
Turkey	
United Kingdom	
West Germany	
Yugoslavia	

In terms of tourist receipts, Italy ranks first, followed by France and Spain. Austria, a relatively small country in terms of area and population, showed in excess of $5 billion in tourist receipts, a figure comparable to much larger countries, such as Great Britain and West Germany. Finally, Spain and, to some extent, Greece play significant roles in shaping the development of charter markets in Europe. In 1984, almost 20 million passengers traveled to and from Spain and about 5 million from Greece using nonscheduled services. These two countries are popular vacation destinations for tourists from Great Britain and West Germany. About half of the total nonscheduled traffic to and from Spain is between Spain and the United Kingdom and about one-fourth between Spain and West Germany.

The European Air Transportation System

Before examining the forces pushing for change in the regulatory environment in Europe, it would be helpful to review the economic, political, and institutional characteristics of the current air transportation system in Europe. This review will assist in gauging the likelihood, type, and extent of changes that can be introduced into the system. This review will also be helpful in evaluating the likelihood and the potential impact of these changes.

Airline Market Structure

In 1985, the airlines registered in Europe accounted for 32.7 percent of the total ton-kilometers in scheduled service worldwide. However, this figure is misleading because of the relatively small size of European nations, which reduces the importance of domestic travel compared to the huge North American domestic market. Consequently, European carriers accounted for 37.5 percent of international operations while European domestic operations accounted for 27.6 percent.[1] Of the top fifty countries in the world whose airlines performed more than 100 million ton-kilometers in scheduled air services in 1985, fourteen are in Europe. Great Britain, France, and West Germany are in fourth, fifth, and sixth place, respectively. In terms of international passenger movements (scheduled and charter), the intra-Europe region is the largest single region in the world, accounting for almost 60 million (37 percent) of the total 162 million passengers. The second and third largest passenger markets in the world are between North America and Europe (18 million passengers in 1985) and between Europe and Africa (14 million passengers in 1985).[2]

The three largest European countries in terms of air travel demand on scheduled services are France, Great Britain, and West Germany. The number of markets with more than 100 passengers per day is considerably more from London (seventy-seven) than from either Paris (forty-one) or Frankfurt (thirty-six). From Frankfurt, nineteen markets are intra-European, eight are to North America, six are to the Asia-Pacific region, two are to Africa, and one is to the Middle East. Only London has more than 1,000 passengers a day from Frankfurt. From London, forty-three markets are intra-European, seventeen are to North America, seven are to the Asia-Pacific region, five are to the Middle East, four are to Africa, and one is to the Caribbean. There are five markets with more than 1,000 passengers per day: Paris, New York, Amsterdam, Dublin, and Frankfurt (in that order). From Paris, twenty-four markets are intra-European, six are to North America, five are to Africa, three are to the Asia-Pacific region, and one each is to the Middle East, Mexico, and South America. There are two markets with more than 1,000 passengers per day: London and New York.

From a financial, political, and operational standpoint, the North Atlantic market is particularly important to European carriers. Between London, Paris, and Frankfurt—the three most important cities in Europe—and cities in North America, scheduled service is available in seventeen markets from London, eight markets from Frankfurt, and six markets from Paris. For many European carriers, their domestic markets are too small to support their large-scale operations, and they rely heavily on the trans-Atlantic traffic. It is in this market that they compete directly against the U.S. carriers, and the competition is fierce. During 1985, North American airlines increased their trans-Atlantic capacity by about 15 percent, compared to about an 11 percent increase for the European carriers. For the North American carriers, the increase in capacity came primarily through the opening of new routes. For the European carriers, the increase in capacity resulted mostly from increases in frequency on existing routes.

In Europe, nonscheduled services account for a much larger percentage of total services than they do in other regions. During 1985 in intra-European international operations, nonscheduled travel accounted for 43 percent of total travel in terms of passengers and 55 percent in terms of passenger-kilometers.[3] Thus, more than half of the total international intra-European passenger-kilometers are performed in nonscheduled service offering discount fares. This attribute continues to have an enormous impact on the market structure, performance, and conduct of the air transportation industry in Europe. For example, not only do scheduled airlines carry charter traffic, but a number of major charter airlines in Europe are subsidiaries of large scheduled airlines. In addition, in Great Britain, West Germany, and other countries, charter operations tend to be regulated to a very small degree compared to scheduled operations. In some of the smaller countries, charter regulations tend to be more restrictive, presumably to protect the scheduled airlines.

Although there are more than 130 airlines in Europe, the lion's share of the passenger traffic to, from, and within Europe is carried by the twenty-one member airlines of the Association of European Airlines (AEA). Scheduled passenger traffic carried by individual member airlines of the AEA in 1986 is shown in table 3–2. British Airways is the largest airline operating into and out of Europe in terms of both passenger-kilometers and number of passengers carried. In 1986, British Airways, Air France, and Lufthansa combined performed 43.5 percent of the passenger-kilometers and carried 37.3 percent of the passengers. Table 3–3 lists the top fifteen nonscheduled airlines in the world, thirteen of which are located in Europe. Many of these airlines are either subsidiaries of or are at least closely associated with the national airlines. Examples include Lufthansa and Condor, British Airways and British

Table 3–2
Scheduled Passenger Traffic Carried by Members of the Association of European Airlines, 1986

	Passenger-Kilometers		Passengers	
Airline	No. (millions)	Percent	No. (thousands)	Percent
Aer Lingus	2,496	1.1	1,972	1.7
Air France	27,571	12.7	12,026	10.1
Alitalia	13,994	6.4	8,383	7.1
Austrian	1,377	0.6	1,495	1.3
British Airways	40,430	18.6	16,998	14.4
BCAL	7,324	3.4	2,381	2.0
Finnair	2,918	1.3	2,897	2.4
Iberia	18,333	8.4	13,593	11.5
Icelandair	2,214	1.0	768	0.6
JAT	4,085	1.9	3,364	2.8
KLM	19,070	8.8	5,074	4.3
Lufthansa	26,645	12.2	15,173	12.8
Luxair	120	0.1	248	0.2
Malev	1,093	0.5	1,151	1.0
Olympic	6,382	2.9	6,480	5.5
SABENA	5,561	2.6	2,233	1.9
SAS	12,539	5.8	11,870	10.0
Swissair	12,874	5.9	6,317	5.3
TAP	4,475	2.0	2,132	1.8
THY	3,049	1.4	2,941	2.5
UTA	5,243	2.4	891	0.8
Total	217,793		118,387	

Source: Association of European Airlines (AEA), *Yearbook 1986* (Brussels: AEA, May 1987), 43.

Airtours, SAS and Scanair, KLM and Martinair, and Air France and Air Charter.

The preeminent positions of France, Great Britain, and West Germany in terms of air travel demand and their national carriers' roles in meeting that demand underscore the importance of the involvement of these countries in the formulation of aviation policy. Two other countries that play an important role in European aviation policy are Spain and, to a smaller extent, Greece, because they are major destinations for passengers using charter services of both scheduled and charter airlines. Spain is by far the largest charter

Table 3–3
International Nonscheduled Airlines and Passenger Traffic, 1984

Airline	Passenger-Kilometers (millions)
Britannia (U.K.)	7,661
Condor (West Germany)	6,672
LTU (West Germany)	6,395
Wardair (Canada)	5,788
British Airtours (U.K.)	4,149
Sterling (Denmark)	3,923
Hapag-Llyod (West Germany)	3,795
Scanair (Scandinavia)	3,436
Monarch (U.K.)	2,858
Air Europe (U.K.)	2,779
Martinair (Netherlands)	2,428
Orion (U.K.)	2,394
American Trans Air (U.S.)	2,347
Air Charter (France)	2,054
Spantax (Spain)	1,928
Total for top 15 carriers	58,607
Total for remaining carriers	16,593
Total for all carriers	75,200

Source: International Civil Aviation Organization (ICAO), *The Economic Situation of Air Transport: Review and Outlook* (Montreal: ICAO, July 1986), 23.

passenger destination within Europe. In 1984, 19.9 million passengers traveled to and from Spain on nonscheduled services compared to 4.4 million on scheduled services.[4]

Characteristics of the European Air Transportation Market

To comprehend the extent to which changes can be introduced in the European regulatory system, it is helpful to keep in mind the characteristics that distinguish the European airline industry from that in other regions in the world. These characteristics include government ownership, government aid, pooling arrangements, labor policies, infrastructural constraints and costs, extensive nonscheduled services, and highly effective and competitive surface transportation facilities. In addition, Europe is a collection of almost two dozen sovereign nations, each with its own national interests and national prestige. Although any of these characteristics alone may not make the European nations unique, as a group, they do set Europe apart from other regions.

The majority of European airlines are completely or partially government-owned, and airlines in Europe, as airlines in many other parts of the world, receive various forms of financial aid from their governments. The purpose, nature, and extent of government aid varies from country to country. Financial assistance is provided: (1) to compensate airlines for the imposition of a public service obligation; (2) to develop and operate domestic services; (3) to provide service to economically underdeveloped regions; (4) to encourage the acquisition and operation of specific airplanes; or (5) simply to cover an airline's operating losses. For example, the Spanish government has given Iberia almost $700 million to cover eight years of accumulated losses. European governments support their national airlines for many reasons: as a token of sovereignty, for international prestige, to serve political routes, to provide jobs, and to generate foreign exchange. Such aid is frequently in the form of direct or indirect capital, loans, or guarantees. In other cases, governments may provide preferential treatment to their national airlines for airport or en-route navigational charges. For example, for a number of years, Olympic (the national airline of Greece) did not pay landing fees at Athens on international flights.[5]

Although the provision of government aid is not a new concept, it has become a significant issue in the liberalization debate. Competition cannot be expected to work effectively unless there are some controls on the amount of government aid available to airlines. Without controls, governments could end up financing competition, and competition would simply become a "subsidy race."[6] The use of government subsidy should not put one airline at a competitive disadvantage relative to another airline. The EEC has proposed that government aid should be transparent and under strict control. The EEC proposal does not prohibit government aid, but it does require the application of well-defined rules to determine the extent and nature of government aid available to an airline. However, the existence of such interference is anathema to a free-market operation.

To reduce the amount of aid paid to national airlines, some countries are trying to transfer a larger percentage of ownership to private entities. In January 1987, the British government sold its ownership in British Airways for almost $1.5 billion. The Dutch government, which owns only about 40 percent of KLM, is planning to decrease its ownership share even further. The Belgian government, which owns about half of SABENA, would like to reduce its share to 27 percent by selling its stock to the public. Governments are moving to privatize their national airlines to control public spending and raise cash and, to a lesser extent, to increase their carriers' productivity and efficiency. Although it is doubtful that many governments (outside the United

States) would relinquish total control of their national-flag carriers—given the importance many governments attach to flag carriers—opening state-owned airlines to private investors could have wide implications, such as a reduction in the operation of unprofitable routes, greater freedom from government-imposed constraints, and a need to earn a more satisfactory return on investment (ROI). The experience of British Airways demonstrates these trends. Prior to the government divestiture, during the early 1980s, the airline reduced its services by 10 percent and its staff by almost 40 percent.

The focus on earnings will become even more critical as the trend toward privatization grows and affects the airplane financing and selection process. Government ownership had a significant influence on the types of airplanes selected by many airlines, and the privatization trend is likely to reduce this politically motivated influence. More directly, the IATA estimates that the financial needs for replacing existing airplanes by the mid-1990s will be up to $200 billion worldwide, but the past financial performance of government-owned airlines has not been adequate to meet the needs of lenders.[7] During 1984 and 1985, the total operations of IATA members produced net profit margins of only 1.5 percent and 1.2 percent, respectively.[8] Whereas, in the past, deficiencies in financial performance were compensated partially by government guarantees, the trend toward privatization—which diminishes the role of the government—will force the airlines to improve their debt/equity ratios and to earn an adequate return on investment. Thus, even in the absence of full deregulation, there are growing economic pressures on some carriers to become more efficient.

The need to improve financial performance may actually lead to the continued practice of pooling arrangements, a characteristic of the European market that protects marginally efficient carriers. On the majority of intra-European routes, there are two primary scheduled airlines (although in some of the larger markets there may be one or more fifth-freedom carriers). In most of the two-carrier cases, there are formal or informal agreements to share the total market between the third- and fourth-freedom carriers. These pooling agreements are normally a condition of operations under bilateral agreements. Pooling of revenue and capacity becomes important when one of the two carriers in the market is weaker than the other. Even when the two carriers are equally strong, pooling can be advantageous by eliminating frequency competition and thereby reducing costs. Typically, revenue is shared in proportion to the share of capacity offered, and some pooling agreements do not have a limit on the amount of revenue that can be transferred between partners. Agreements that do limit the amount of revenue that can be transferred provide some incentive for an aggressive partner that is more successful in selling its capacity. From the passenger's point of view, pooled frequencies theoretically can lead to more rationalized schedules than would be available if the two carriers competitively scheduled flights during peak periods only.

Recognizing that pooling arrangements eliminate competitive incentives—at least when there is no limit to the amount of revenue that can be transferred between partners—the proponents of increased liberalization are urging governments (1) to make pooling of revenue and capacity an option, not a requirement, in the bilateral agreement; (2) not to insist on a rigid fifty-fifty share of traffic; and (3) to impose lower transfer limits. The EEC (in its *Civil Aviation Memorandum No. 2*) proposed a system of capacity freedom within predetermined parameters. Under this proposal, one government could not take action against the airline of another country unless the percentage of traffic carried by its own airline fell below 25 percent of the total third- and fourth-freedom traffic carried between the two countries by the two airlines. Subsequently, the trigger point was raised to 45 percent. The limit proposed on revenue transfers was one percent. Although the European airlines generally did not oppose the concepts of the EEC proposal, they did object to the actual parameters on the grounds that they were arbitrary. In their view, it is more important to establish policies that promote traffic on the basis of fair and equal opportunities rather than to establish policies that simply replace one set of rigid rules for another set of rigid rules, even if the new rules contain different limits.[9] Despite attempts to liberalize pooling agreements, the existence of such arrangements in any form is contrary to the doctrine of free-market determination and is a powerful force against European deregulation.

Fundamentally dissimilar labor structures are another obstacle to the implementation of U.S.-style deregulation. Typically, European labor costs are about 30 percent of total costs for scheduled international operations, roughly comparable to the postderegulation labor-cost ratios of the U.S. carriers. However, they are significantly higher than labor-cost ratios of most carriers based in the Asia-Pacific region (notable exceptions are Qantas and Japan Airlines). In the Asia-Pacific region, even including Japan Airlines and Qantas, labor costs average just 15 percent of total costs.[10] Consequently, the European airlines operate at a substantial competitive disadvantage relative to most airlines based in the Asia-Pacific region. And although, in the past, the European carriers operated at comparable or occasionally lower costs than U.S. carriers, the European airlines are now at a competitive disadvantage even to the U.S. carriers. In the United States, deregulation allowed airline managements to negotiate lower labor rates and higher productivity levels. This action has not been possible because of the regulatory framework and the highly unionized labor force within Europe. In this context, it is quite possible that a number of the European governments and/or airlines may be promoting the idea of regulatory reforms with the objective of reducing labor costs indirectly.

Of course, the wage level itself is only one component of unit labor; the other component is labor productivity. Although it is very difficult to compare labor productivity among airlines because of the differences among airlines' operations and route networks and the degree of outside contract work, use of the simplistic measure of available ton-kilometers per employee shows that the European airlines are once again at a disadvantage relative to a number of carriers based in the United States and the Asia-Pacific region. European airlines are being constrained by such institutional factors as social labor laws and greater government bureaucracy, resulting in higher labor costs and lower labor productivity. Even though such labor practices hinder European carriers in global markets, it seems incongruous that some socialistic governments of Europe, which are committed to job creation, would be willing to accept U.S.-style deregulation inasmuch as airline employees have been the big losers of U.S. airline deregulation.

Just as flag carriers of Europe have had to contend with the socialistic labor practices imposed on them by their owner governments, so too have they been severely handicapped by the inadequacy and high cost of infrastructural facilities in Europe. These inadequacies relate both to the physical capacity of various entities (such as airports) and to "the procedural and political difficulties at local, national, and international levels within and between the components of the industry and their operating agencies."[11] Many European governments have imposed burdensome controls that affect airline operations and costs. For example, extensive customs and immigration procedures and excessive documentation result in costly airplane departure delays. According to the Association of European Airlines, European infrastructural costs are among the highest in the world. In 1984, these costs represented as much as 11 percent of the total costs of European airlines operating scheduled service within Europe.[12] Worldwide, the average user charges are about 5 percent of total costs.[13] High user charges exist in Europe for two reasons. First, European airlines incur a higher proportion of landing fees because of short stage lengths. Second, Eurocontrol imposes charges for the use of airspace in western Europe. Unlike their U.S. counterparts, European carriers are assessed user fees to cover the costs of en-route and airport navigation facilities. Each country maintains its own navigation and air traffic control facilities, and the user fees are a function of the weight of the airplane and the distance flown across the airspace of an individual country. In the United States, such facilities are provided by the FAA and are paid for, in part, by a passenger tax on airline tickets.

Although the facility use fees are paid by all users—and, in theory, no group of carriers has an advantage over any other—the European airlines claim that these user charges do affect their competitive positions relative to other modes of transportation over comparable distances. So far, no proposals have been presented to remedy the high cost of using inadequate infrastructual facilities. The EEC's *Memorandum No. 2* simply stated that the EEC would develop a proposal for the establishment and implementation of common principles for user charges.

It is also important to keep in mind that, in Europe, other transportation modes are viable competitors to air travel because of relatively small intra-continental distances and high population density. Rail transportation, in particular, is successful because Europe has one of the most extensive, most effective, and best railroad systems in the world. It is most extensive in that about one-third of the world's total railroad track lies in Europe, and parts of it carry express trains. It is most effective in that Europe's population centers are extremely condensed compared to those of other continents. And it is one of the best as measured by quality of ride, cruising speed, interconnected network, and frequency of service. The trans-Europe express trains, traveling at about 100 miles per hour, link the major cities in nine western European nations. The French TGV (Train à Grande Vitesse) cruises at almost 170 miles per hour between Paris and Lyon. Major cities in West Germany receive hourly train service. Finally, it must be pointed out that the European rail service is heavily subsidized. In addition, automobile travel still accounts for a major share of passenger travel in Europe, given the shorter hauls relative to the United States, the high number of cars per unit of population, the extensive network of highways, and the ease of border crossings. Thus, the quality and quantity of surface transportation has a major impact on the air mode's share of passenger travel.

The foregoing attributes of European air transportation, particularly when taken as a group, provide a set of conflicting forces to the liberalization movement. And governments fully recognize that any benefits of reduced regulation must exceed the costs, both direct and indirect. For example, a more liberalized environment could reduce labor force levels at existing major carriers. On the other hand, beneficial as it may be in terms of reducing labor costs, such a policy would clearly run against the ideologies of some socialist governments. Similarly, an increase in competition clearly would weed out the inefficient carriers; yet very few governments would allow their national airlines to go bankrupt, no matter how inefficient they are. Thus, it is in the context of these conflicting pressures on governments that one must evaluate the degree to which changes can be expected in the European airline industry.

Fares

The level of fares within Europe is frequently criticized when European fares are compared to fares available in other parts of the world, particularly in the United States and on the North Atlantic. Table 3–4 shows the level of normal economy class passenger fares on local European routes, disaggregated into six distance blocks. The data shown in this table include all routes between or among the countries of geographic Europe, Algeria, the Azores, Canary Islands, Greenland, Iceland, Madeira, Malta, Morocco, Tunisia, and Turkey. During September 1985, the normal economy fares were higher than

Table 3–4
Comparison of Local European and World Normal Economy Fares per Passenger-Kilometer, September 1985

Route Group	Cents/Passenger-Kilometer by Distance (km)				
	250	500	1,000	2,000	4,000
Europe	36.3	27.9	21.5	16.6	12.8
Int'l total—world	28.7	23.6	19.4	16.0	13.2
Europe as a percentage of world	126	118	111	104	97

Source: International Civil Aviation Organization (ICAO), *Survey of International Air Transport Fares and Rates, September 1985* (Montreal: ICAO, June 1986), 16.

the average for all routes in the world for all distance groups, except routes with distances equal to or more than 4,000 kilometers. The ICAO analysis was based on 2,310 city pairs in Europe. The majority of the city pairs (964, or 41.7 percent) fell in the distance group between 1,000 and 1,999 kilometers.[14] For this group, the normal economy fares were about 11 percent higher than the world average.

The basic premise underlying the desire for change is the hypothesis that the higher fares in Europe relative to other regions of the world are the result of an imperfect market that (1) provides excessive profits for the carriers, (2) protects inefficient carriers, or (3) allows airlines to cross-subsidize between price-inelastic and price-elastic travelers. Since European carriers as a group have not reported excessively large returns on investment—and assuming that cross-subsidization is minimal—champions of change argue that inefficient operating practices have become ingrained in European carriers. The deregulators then continue to say that if the only *real* difference between the airlines in Europe and North America is the regulatory environment in which the two groups of airlines operate, then it is time to change that regulatory environment to provide the desired benefits for both producers and users of air transportation services.

The logic of the foregoing argument for deregulation rests squarely on the assumption that not only are European fares higher than those in other parts of the world, but they would come down appreciably even if the industry were only partially deregulated. Although there is no question that the industry would become more efficient from an economic point of view, it is debatable whether the level of fares would come down to any significant degree. Typical comparisons made in the media tend to be misleading in that they are comparing apples to oranges. The most misleading analyses are those that contrast normal economy fares within Europe with the lowest available fares in the United States in markets of comparable distance. These fare comparisons lose sight of the fact that not only do operating conditions vary from region to region, but fares are related to characteristics of the service provided. The most important difference, however, relates to the cost of operations. Operating costs are a function of network and market characteristics, and they also vary from region to region because of the differences in such cost categories as aircraft size, price of fuel, level of user charges, and marketing costs. In 1984, the total operating costs in Europe per passenger-kilometer were 12.1 cents, compared to 6.96 cents for all international operations worldwide. (See Table 2–11.) Once adjustments are made for cost variations, a large percentage of the differences in the level of European fares and the levels of U.S. domestic fares and North Atlantic fares can be explained by the differences in operating costs. The EEC reached this conclusion in its *Civil Aviation Memorandum No. 2*. Even if these conclusions are accepted, the proponents of change then point out, correctly, that European fares reflect costs that are excessive because of inefficiencies built into the system as a result of lack of competition. Opponents, of course, do not agree with the hypothesis that differences in fares equal differences in costs. They claim that whereas cost differences between the United States and Europe are about 20 percent, fare differences average between 35 and 40 percent, leaving a sufficient margin to be reduced by additional competition.[15]

Critics claim that there is no price competition. Again, this criticism is not strictly accurate. First, although price competition among scheduled carriers has been minimal, it does exist between scheduled and charter carriers that offer package vacations. These charter airlines have played a role similar to the one played by the U.S. no-frill carrier, People Express. Since more than half of the total demand for air travel is satisfied by the nonscheduled services, it is totally unreasonable to assume that there is no competition. Second, in a number of major markets, scheduled service is provided by fifth-freedom carriers, some of which enjoy low operating costs. These carriers, partly because of their lower costs and partly because of their need to fill up excess capacity, have been able to introduce some fare competition. Finally, as has already been discussed, other modes of transportation (railroads, cars, and buses) provide effective and viable forms of competition for the airline industry in Europe.

In the past, passengers had a choice of buying scheduled services from legitimate sources and paying higher fares or buying the same services in the "gray market" for considerably lower fares. Alternatively, passengers could use nonscheduled services, which charged lower fares. About half of the traveling public purchased tickets, directly or indirectly, for travel on scheduled airlines, while the other half used nonscheduled services of either scheduled airlines or charter airlines. Assuming that the EEC's conclusions about the level of European fares are reasonable, the issue, then, is not whether a more liberalized environment for establishing, approving, and implementing fares will produce lower fares. Rather, the hypothesis is that a more liberalized environment (1) would legitimize the lower fares that, in the past, had to be obtained through indirect sources and (2) would encourage scheduled airlines to produce a wider range of fares. The variety of fares offered by scheduled airlines has been limited, except in certain markets. There is strong pressure to change the procedures for fixing air fares such that scheduled airlines will offer a much broader spectrum of price/service options, similar to the situation in the United States. Thus, deregulation—to the extent that it is implemented—is likely to lead not to lower fares but to a wider range of fares available directly from scheduled airlines and their normal channels of distribution. At present, the average fare on scheduled services is about 40 percent below the normal economy fares and about 60 percent of passengers are making use of available discount fares.

In the past, international fares for scheduled services were almost always jointly determined at the IATA traffic conferences and approved by the respective governments. From time to time, some difficulties were encountered in reaching a compromise. For the most part, however, the airlines did agree on acceptable tariffs. In general, deviations from the agreed tariffs were small, although a few carriers did practice illegal discounting at the risk of being fined. However, discounting through "bucket shops" has been a relatively common phenomenon, and the widespread availability of such discount fares is a valid argument for liberalization, in that it would legitimize these de facto fares.

Legitimization of the gray market is not the only argument for revamping the European fare-fixing system. During the past decade, the changing characteristics of the market have had a very persuasive influence on pricing policies. First, the composition of the travel market changed as more and more people in lower income brackets began to travel for personal and pleasure reasons. Since this segment of the market is more price-sensitive, the "bucket shop" operations mushroomed. Second, the composition of the airlines that provide service to Europeans has also changed. There are now large carriers that not only operate outside the IATA traffic conference machinery but are more cost-efficient and more marketing-oriented, and many are based in the high-growth Asia-Pacific region. Third, increased competition is challenging the airlines to better manage their capacity as a means of increasing revenues. For these three reasons alone, the need to introduce innovative fares has increased. However, the traditional airline distribution system was not capable of handling a flexible tariff environment. Computerized reservation systems that can accommodate instantaneous tariff changes have only recently replaced cumbersome printed schedules. Under the old system, there was no way for the airlines to publicize fares that would appeal to a changing market.

With the advent of automation, an innovative tariff approach has been under the spotlight in recent years—the concept of the "zone of reasonableness." In 1982, the United States and the ECAC agreed to establish a fare system based on this concept for North Atlantic operations, a market that accounts for about 25 percent of the world's total international air traffic. Under this fare system, airlines receive automatic government approval for all fares that fall within the zone. The underlying premise is that an individual airline can change its fares quickly to meet market conditions while still maintaining a price floor and ceiling, designed to protect the flag carriers and consumers, respectively. In addition, this system reduces the administrative burden on governments with respect to the fare approval process and allows different airlines to fulfill different objectives in pricing policies. The basic reference fares have been adjusted annually to reflect changes in airline operating costs, such as recent adjustments for lower fuel prices. Forced by the actions of the EEC, the European countries are now adopting a similar zone concept within Europe as part of the liberalization movement.

Airlines with sophisticated yield management capability should be in a position to exploit the zone concept to improve their bottom line and, at the same time, to provide fares that are more responsive to the needs of the marketplace. Based on the experience of the U.S. carriers in recent years, it is clear that an airline can increase its revenue and profits by controlling more judiciously the distribution of its seat inventories—that is, the percentage of seats sold at different fares. Although, in the past, 75 to 85 percent of the revenue from incremental passengers contributed to profits, it is now recognized that upgrading certain passengers within the same class of service can contribute an even higher percentage of revenue to profits. In most cases the only additional expenses associated with transporting a higher-paying passenger within the same class of service is the additional commission cost. Whereas past regulatory constraints and antiquated distribution systems could not quickly accommodate implementation of a broad spectrum of fares to meet the changing needs of the marketplace, the zone concept should eliminate this obstacle. The extent to which each airline can take advantage of this opportunity will depend heavily on the degree of sophistication an airline can incorporate in its yield management process and procedures, which depends, in turn, on the financial resources the carrier can commit to the development and maintenance of these costly systems. The importance of automated systems and their impact on a carrier's market performance are evidenced by the growing dispute over alleged bias in computerized reservation systems. As in the United States, this is expected to be an ongoing dispute.

Actual fares—as well as the procedures for developing and implementing fares in Europe and on the North Atlantic—have been under review for some time because of numerous changes in the marketplace. Assuming that many of the European governments will remain interested in some form of fare regulation for such reasons as the need to provide equal opportunity for airlines and to reduce the possibility of predatory or discriminatory fares, it would appear that some form of the IATA fare-setting system will continue. However, modifications are likely to be introduced in the multilateral fare negotiation and implementation system. Airlines could be provided with the basic criteria for setting fares, including such provisions as relationship to costs, currency conversions, prorating of revenues, and consumer protection. Second, the multilaterally agreed fares could be used as reference fares that may be amended by individual airlines, a policy similar to the one presently advocated by countries such as Australia and Singapore. Since these types of guidelines can easily be accommodated by the zone concept—while preserving a certain amount of control by the governmental agencies—it is almost certain that the zone concept for fare regulation will be adopted more widely. Acceptance of the zone concept as the pricing mechanism for intra-European travel would not represent complete deregulation. Accordingly, the average fare would not drop significantly; but when it is coupled with efficacious yield management techniques, the zone concept will produce a broader spectrum of legitimate fares, which will be mutually beneficial to airlines and passengers.

The Liberalization Movement

Although changes in the European regulatory regime have been under consideration for a number of years, the pace of the movement, now called the liberalization movement, has accelerated in the mid-1980s, partly in reaction to the initial U.S. experience. However, despite the accelerated pace of the liberalization movement in certain quarters, Europe remains divided on the liberalization issue. At one end of the spectrum are the procompetitive governments: the Benelux countries and the United Kingdom. (However, even the strongest European advocates of a more procompetitive environment are not suggesting complete elimination of regulatory control, as exemplified by the United Kingdom's desire to control capacity on the North Atlantic.) At the other end of the spectrum are the least procompetitive countries: Spain, Portugal, and Greece. Other countries are in the middle, but they tend to align themselves with one extreme or the other: West Germany and Switzerland are slightly more liberal; others, such as France and the Scandinavian countries, are much more conservative. The tide, however, is turning toward a more liberal environment relative to the previously overconstrained environment as a result of pressure from four major forces: consumer groups, charter and regional airlines, individual nations, and multilaterial entities such as the ECAC, the EEC, and the European Court of Justice. Although each set of forces has contributed to turning this tide, it is the actions of some countries, individually and bilaterally, that will ultimately bring about a reduction in the amount and type of regulation within Europe.

Consumer groups in some parts of Europe are increasingly critical of the quantity, quality, and price of air services. The seriousness of this criticism is debatable for some of the reasons cited earlier. Not only have the EEC studies already shown that scheduled passenger fares are not so high relative to operating costs in Europe, but more than 50 percent of the air travel in Europe is on charter airlines, which offer substantially lower fares than those of scheduled carriers. Moreover, a significant percentage of the traveling public is able to purchase service on scheduled airlines through the gray market. Nevertheless, politicians are under growing public pressure to change the regulatory regime to allow implementation of broader price/service options, if not lower fares.

Regional and charter airlines have provided the second force behind the liberalization movement in Europe. In the larger European nations with high population densities, there is enormous pressure from the smaller airlines to offer service from their regional airports to other European capitals on large aircraft. In general, the smaller regional airlines began service with fares slightly lower than those offered by the incumbent carriers. For example, Ryanair, a small Irish carrier, recently began service between Dublin and Luton airport (north of London) with unrestricted fares using BAe HS-748s. Initially, the fares were set 50 percent below the fares charged by the two incumbent carriers (British Airways and Aer Lingus). The proliferation of smaller regional airlines is not restricted to the secondary routes in international markets. New airlines are making significant inroads in domestic markets also. The national airlines are facing new competition on domestic routes in countries such as France, Great Britain, and Italy.

Charter airlines are also lobbying for access to richer markets and for the freedom to add flights in existing markets. Transavia, a Dutch charter airline, recently began scheduled service between London's Gatwick airport and Amsterdam at fares 50 percent below the prevailing fares. In addition, a number of charter airlines have been increasing their "seat-only" business. Nonscheduled airlines in Europe have traditionally offered inclusive tour packages that include air transportation and land arrangements, such as hotels. A number of these airlines are now interested in selling air transportation only.

The incumbent scheduled carriers are, of course, defending their market share with every weapon available. Their immediate response, naturally, is to lower fares, presumably on a capacity-controlled basis. Another strategy has been to divert group tour business from nonscheduled airlines. In some cases, the incumbent carriers have even resorted to appeals to their governments to slow the expansion of new airlines. For example, it is alleged that the incumbent carriers put pressure on their governments to halt the growth of Ryanair in the Luton–Dublin market. And it is reported that Ryanair did encounter obstacles in obtaining permission to upgrade its equipment to jet aircraft. Incumbent carriers are not the only entities to bring pressure on governments to restrict the growth of new carriers. In July 1986, Air France workers went on strike to protest the French government's decision to authorize two charter airlines to provide scheduled service in competition with Air France.

Multilateral entities such as the ECAC, the EEC, and the European Court of Justice represent the third force behind the liberalization movement. The twenty-two-nation European Civil Aviation Conference has been working toward proposals for liberalization with respect to (1) tariff zones for intra-European routes, (2) reductions in the rigidity of bilateral capacity shares, and (3) a more liberal approach to the development of regional services and market access. The changes contained in the ECAC proposals have been less radical than those contained in the EEC proposals. For example, the ECAC proposed that capacity should not be controlled (nor intervention from governments introduced) until a bilateral partner's share falls below 45 percent. The EEC's initial proposal was more radical, since it limited a bilateral partner's share to 25 percent. In the area of tariffs, the ECAC recommended implementation of a zone concept similar to the one in operation on the North Atlantic. In general, ECAC proposals for regulatory change tend to be less controversial and politically more acceptable, partly because this organization must take into account the interests of twenty-two countries, as opposed to the twelve members of the EEC.

The EEC is fully committed to deregulating the European airline industry to the extent possible by applying the Treaty of Rome's antitrust rules to air travel within the Community. The ultimate goal of the EEC is to develop a European Community policy for commercial air transport to supersede the rules on airline operation that are presently controlled by bilateral aviation agreements and that are the same for both EEC and non-EEC countries. Although there is significant pressure from the EEC to introduce greater liberalization, there are two constraints. First, despite the EEC's enthusiasm, the desire for and the extent of change vary significantly among the members of the Community, with Greece at one extreme and the Netherlands at the other. Second, the likelihood of the EEC's proposals becoming a reality across the whole region is relatively small, since they do not reflect the views of the non-EEC countries.

The EEC's initial contribution was the development of the Regional Air Services Directive, encouraging air services between the Community's regional airports. The pressure to develop such an initiative came from the United Kingdom. Although the original EEC proposal would have made substantial progress, the final directive became far less liberal as a result of the changes introduced by countries with restrictionist policies. The EEC proposed a number of other measures, in its *Memorandum No. 1*, to improve the market structure within Europe, consistent with the directives of the Treaty of Rome.[16] Many of the proposed measures were considered too radical and therefore politically unacceptable. Partly because of the unacceptability of *Memorandum No. 1* (as originally presented), the EEC's *Memoran-*

dum No. 2 was drafted more conservatively, with an eye toward acceptability. Consequently, *Memorandum No. 2* has exerted some pressure to bring about major changes.

Although it is difficult to envision radical regulatory reforms being implemented as a result of coercion from the EEC alone, some progress is being made toward a more flexible system. The EEC is lobbying the conservative nations (such as Denmark, France, Greece, Portugal, and Spain) to liberalize at least the most restrictive elements in the air services agreements, one at a time. Second, the agreement by the twelve nations in the EEC to sign the European Single Act could facilitate the liberalization movement despite the opposition of some countries. Under this act, a proposal to increase competition within the EEC can be approved by a majority vote. Article 13 of the act also calls for the establishment of an internal market—an area without internal frontiers in which goods, persons, services, and capital can move freely. Moreover, the EEC is also beginning to flex its muscles by threatening, first, to withdraw its temporary exemption of the airlines from the Community's competition rules and, second, to take legal action in the European Court of Justice against airlines that continue anticompetitive practices.

On its part, the European Court of Justice recently nudged the liberalization movement a little further by its decision in the Nouvelles Frontières (a French travel agent and tour operator) case. In this case, the travel agency appealed to the European Court for having been penalized by the French government for selling tickets to the United States and Southeast Asia at prices below the official IATA-approved rates. On April 30, 1986, the European Court reached the following decision: The EEC's antitrust rules (articles 85-90 of the Treaty of Rome) do apply to airlines operating in the EEC, even though there are no specific Community regulations governing air travel. The ramifications of this decision could be significant in that this decision (1) gives the EEC the power to sue airlines in breach of the Treaty of Rome's antitrust rules and (2) could force the EEC authorities and the governments of member states to decide about Community regulations.

The fourth and most significant force behind the liberalization movement comes from a small group of individual countries that are not satisfied with the rate at which multilateral initiatives are being taken. These countries are pushing the liberalization movement on both unilateral and bilateral bases. The United Kingdom is at the forefront of the liberalization movement in western Europe. Its interest is motivated by a large home-base traffic, a large domestic market, a large number and variety of British airlines, a very strong consumer movement, a favorable attitude of the government toward a competitive system, and strong support from the two largest national carriers (British Airways and British Caledonian). Consequently, the British government has been very active in increasing competition in domestic and international markets. It is interesting to note that in its decision to privatize British Airways, its flag carrier, the British government had to streamline the carrier's operations and improve its financial structure to make it attractive for privatization. This process involved the elimination of 26,000 jobs, but British Airways is now positioned to take advantage of the changing market environment. The Netherlands is another strong advocate of a competitive regime, presumably because its home market is small relative to the size of its flag carrier (KLM) and because KLM has been positioned for some time to benefit from a more competitive environment. The United Kingdom and the Netherlands, while waiting for other countries to make up their minds on the liberalization issue, decided in 1984 to renegotiate their own bilateral air services agreement to make it as liberal as possible.

Partly because of the initial favorable outcome (that is, growth in traffic) of the new bilateral agreement between the United Kingdom and the Netherlands, the Belgian and West German governments shifted their policies to move closer to the views of the liberal governments. West Germany has traditionally followed a conservative aviation policy, but it accepted country-of-origin tariff rules. The shift in West Germany's aviation policy probably is also based on the fact that its flag carrier (Lufthansa) is a strong carrier that could capitalize on emerging opportunities in a liberalized environment. There has even been a change in French attitudes since the election of a right-wing government. There are strong indications that the French government is more willing to allow free-market forces to dictate aviation policy.

The foregoing developments have forced even the nations and carriers that are exceptionally slow to adapt to the changing environment to at least become concerned with the impact of the movement on their nations and their national carriers. The reasons for their concern include public pressure (as in France), high costs (such as SAS), poor financial performance (such as Iberia and TAP), unprofitable domestic operations (as in Greece), and nations with a peripheral geographic location (such as Finland). Because of these concerns, some traditionally conservative governments are reevaluating their positions to determine the actions they should take to fulfill their national goals. Even when they do not support the liberalization movement, these conservative governments are taking certain actions to position their carriers to survive in the new environment, if not to take advantage of emerging opportunities. The new French government has approved more competition for its flag carrier (for instance, new airlines on domestic routes and UTA on the North Atlantic), and it has made some gestures toward privatizing main national commercial enterprises, such as Air France. The Italian government has agreed to introduce competition on its major domestic route, Milan–Rome. Denmark recently authorized low-fare service on the North Atlantic by a small U.S. airline and a major Danish tour operator. Last year, the Greek government put a halt to the expansion plans of its national carrier until it rationalizes its operations.

As a result of the foregoing developments, some airlines and some governments have started preparing for a less regulated environment (though not a truly competitive marketplace, as in the United States). For example, Air France has been introducing lower fares on routes, has been opening up low-traffic-density routes out of Paris, and has been providing service from provincial cities by chartering airplanes from regional carriers. In the United Kingdom, BCAL attempted to diversify its operations to reposition itself, as exemplified by discussions with the International Leisure Group (Intasun)—the United Kingdom's second largest tour operator—to pool airplanes. Then, BCAL entered into an agreement with SABENA to operate a joint daily Brussels–London–Atlanta flight with a B-747. Finally, BCAL agreed to merge with British Airways. Iberia is trying to attract more business travelers as a way of bolstering its yields, which have been about 30 percent lower than other European carriers.

It is evident from the points raised thus far that there are varying degrees of interest in a more liberal regulatory regime in Europe, although there is no consensus on the method or the degree of liberalization. The inability to formulate aviation policies that would lead to a more liberal environment is the result of air transport characteristics unique to this region and the divergent social, economic, and political situations of key European states. It is ironic that some multilateral organizations are attempting to push forward the idea of an air transport "common market," when it has not even been possible to agree on a common definition of Europe. Nonetheless, there is agreement that neither U.S.-style deregulation nor the status quo are acceptable. What, then, are the changes that are likely to be accepted? And what are the consequences of such changes? The next section suggests a plausible set of changes to the regulatory system that would simultaneously promote competitive practices to increase efficiency, preserve the desired features of the old system, and protect, to a limited extent, the national interests of various governments and their national airlines.

Future Prospects

Although most European governments recognize that the airline industry could achieve greater economic and social efficiency by restructuring the regulatory framework, there is no consensus on what the air transport policy should be. Almost everyone agrees that the present bilateral system should be preserved to maintain the consumer benefits of international cooperation (for instance, interlining). The bilateral mechanism also serves as a sort of financial safety net for governments to protect the interests of their airlines. Unfortunately, these formal agreements are not responsive to sudden changes in market demand, and their inflexibility implies that the European regulatory system system will be changed gradually. However, the progressive attitudes of some governments (as exemplified by the 1984 agreement between the United Kingdom and the Netherlands) have already exposed some airlines to the challenges of the free market. Thus, even though the majority of governments favor an incremental and moderate relaxation of regulatory controls, the liberalization efforts of a few influential governments will nudge the other European governments to act if they hope to sustain the economic viability of their airlines.

The net result of these conflicting forces acting for and against liberalization will be a gradual but irresistible movement toward greater flexibility. Indeed, the process is already well under way. The four sets of forces described earlier are dragging major but traditionally conservative governments, such as France and West Germany, in the direction of a more flexible environment. As this group reluctantly adopts the practices of more liberal governments, the truly conservative nations—such as Italy, Spain, and Portugal—which have gradually agreed to "controlled competition," will have to move further, though by no means all the way, toward a more laissez-faire system. Under this scenario, a controlled-competition system is the first phase of the liberalization process; it is characterized by the development of regional services, wider acceptance and implementation of the zone concept for tariffs, and more freedom in bilateral agreements for capacity deviations and pooling arrangements, especially with respect to the division of revenue. As the liberalization movement gains momentum, the controlled-competition system will evolve into a slightly more procompetitive system.

However, it is not so much the four sets of forces described earlier but the imminent threat of substantial incursions by the U.S. megacarriers (with their gigantic domestic feed, sophisticated computerized reservation systems, and lower labor costs) and the Asia-Pacific carriers (with their low costs, new airplanes, aggressive pricing policies, and high-quality service) that will dictate reasonably quick and decisive action by the European carriers to move into the second phase of regulatory reform—namely, consolidation. This second phase will begin with the leading carriers taking on attributes of efficient megacarriers, operating with more commercially oriented objectives. The formation of European megacarriers will begin, presumably, with mergers among the carriers of the same nation (as was the case between BOAC and BEA in the United Kingdom and the recently announced merger between British Airways and BCAL). Subsequently, this process could be expanded to countries within the same sphere of influence.

This two-step process toward the development of a more procompetitive air transportation system in Europe began to take shape during the early 1980s. The Netherlands and its national airline, KLM, have been the leading promoters of an "open skies" regime for a long time. Their cause was embraced by Prime Minister Thatcher's administration, which ordered British

Airways to become an effective competitor in the freer marketplace. Next, the West German government, which owns about 75 percent of its flag carrier, Lufthansa, began to prepare it for competition against the North American and revamped European megacarriers as well as against the "mean and lean" carriers from the Asia-Pacific region. The preeminent position of these three major carriers (British Airways, Lufthansa, and KLM) and the growing inroads made by the U.S. megacarriers are exerting enormous competitive pressures on other European airlines. They, in turn, are exploring alternative strategies for surviving under the new regime. Scandinavia's SAS exemplifies this trend.

Under the foregoing scenario, the European airline system will eventually take on many, but not all, attributes of the U.S. system, such as more regional airlines initially; mergers, resulting in a concentration of market share in the hands of about half a dozen megacarriers; expansion of the hub-and-spoke system; increasing pressure on airlines to reduce their operating costs; increasing commuter-type operations, with linkages to the major airlines; a broader spectrum of price/service options; and a decline in the share of the traffic carried by charter airlines. However, unlike the United States, in which inefficient medium-sized and smaller airlines went out of business, it is doubtful that very many European governments will allow their national carriers to go bankrupt. Some carriers may be forced to reduce the scale of their operations and possibly to become even more dependent on their governments. Some may be forced to merge with other domestic carriers. And in some cases, mergers may take place among international airlines, resulting in multinational entities along the lines of SAS. Mergers among European international airlines will, of course, be complicated processes because of the interplay of economic, political, and social considerations. It is also plausible that some mergers-acquisitions may take place even between European and North American carriers, depending on the degree to which U.S. rules regarding foreign ownership are relaxed. Since some governments would want to maintain independent flag carriers, inefficient national airlines may be forced to scale back operations rather than developing joint operations or mergers. This would be a substantial departure from the U.S. experience, which generally has been merger or failure.

The larger European carriers are concerned with the increasing competition from the U.S. megacarriers, both on the North Atlantic and in the high-yield intra-European markets in which the U.S. airlines have fifth-freedom traffic rights. North Atlantic operations generally constitute a larger proportion of the major European carriers' total operations than of the U.S. carriers' operations. Inasmuch as the U.S. carriers enjoy some advantages mentioned earlier, the European carriers are taking other measures to protect their market shares. They are asking for greater access to the U.S. markets and additional rights to points beyond their U.S. gateways that would parallel rights of U.S. carriers beyond their gateway points in Europe; they are increasing frequency, particularly in direct and nonstop service; and they are combining operations to become stronger competitors. Some of the larger European carriers are even considering taking equity positions in U.S. regional carriers to improve their traffic feed.

One constant complaint of the European carriers is that they do not have cabotage rights in the United States. Some members of the EEC have even pointed to this weakness as a reason for establishing a common air transport market in Europe. Whereas, in the past, a number of European nations have been reluctant to surrender their sovereign negotiation rights and have, instead, wanted to develop their own markets, the proliferation of multinational airlines, the concept of an internal market (article 13 of the Single European Act), the growing incursions of U.S. megacarriers in Europe, and the U.S. reluctance to give cabotage traffic rights may yet lead to the establishment of a common European air transport market.

In summary, the forthcoming changes in the regulation of the European airline industry will change the market structure, performance, and conduct in this industry. These changes are partly the result of movements in Europe to make the system more flexible and partly the result of the threat from the U.S. megacarriers. The new environment will probably increase concentration in the airline industry, and the surviving carriers will be more efficient, more opportunistic, less dependent on their governments, less tolerant of government interference in management decisions, more responsive to their customers, and better positioned to compete with the carriers from North America and the Asia-Pacific region. As for the passengers, they are not so likely to see exceptionally low fares, but they *are* likely to see a much broader spectrum of price/service options offered by scheduled airlines. Just as the changes in the U.S. regulatory regime are producing changes in the European airline industry, some of the same changes in the European system could produce changes in the Middle East, the subject of the next chapter.

Notes

1. International Civil Aviation Organization (ICAO), *Bulletin* (Montreal: ICAO, June 1986), 25.

2. International Air Transport Association (IATA), *World Air Transport Statistics, 1985* (Geneva: IATA, June 1986), 30.

3. International Civil Aviation Organization (ICAO), *The Economic Situation of Air Transport: Review and Outlook* (Montreal: ICAO, 1986), 22.

4. Stephen Wheatcroft and Geoffrey Lipman, *Air Transport in a Competitive European Market* (London: The Economist, 1986), 22.

5. Rigas Doganis, *Flying Off Course: The Economics of International Airlines* (London: George Allen & Unwin, 1985), 104.

6. Commission of the European Communities, *Civil Aviation Memorandum No. 2: Progress Towards the Development of a Community Air Transport Policy* (Brussels: EEC, 15 March 1984), 36.

7. International Air Transport Association, *IATA Annual Report 1986* (Geneva: IATA, November 1986), 5.

8. Ibid.

9. Association of European Airlines (AEA), *EEC Air Transport Policy: AEA Views* (Brussels: AEA, July 1984).

10. Doganis, *Flying Off Course,* 90.

11. Commission of the European Communities, *Memorandum No. 2,* 41.

12. AEA, *EEC Air Transport Policy,* 29.

13. Doganis, *Flying Off Course,* 102.

14. International Civil Aviation Organization (ICAO), *Survey of International Air Transport Fares and Rates, September 1985* (Montreal: ICAO, June 1986).

15. "Europe's Air Cartel," *The Economist,* 1 November 1986, 24.

16. Commission of the European Communities, *Contributions of the European Communities to the Development of Air Transport Service: Memorandum to the Commission* (Brussels: EEC, 6 July 1979).

4
The Middle East

The market structure, performance, and operating practices of airlines based in the Middle East have been substantially influenced by the region's geographic importance, contentious rivalries, and the volatility of oil prices over the past decade and a half. For centuries, the Middle East has been a mercantile center for East–West trade, and its location as a natural link between East and West is now a stimulus to the air transportation industry. On the other hand, this region has a long history of political tension, and unsettling events of the past few years, which have affected tourism and the distribution of oil wealth, have also severely damaged a number of Middle Eastern airlines (primarily those in Lebanon, Iraq, and Iran). However, the cyclical rise and subsequent decline of petroleum revenues has been the prime determinant of airline policies among the region's carriers.

Since 1973, a number of airlines in this region have gone through a substantial expansion phase relative to other parts of the world, due in large part to the robust vitality of some of the region's economies. The expansionary policies are now being carefully reconsidered in view of falling petroleum revenues and the resultant drop in economic prosperity. These airlines are particularly vulnerable to a prolonged contraction because, despite the increase in the demand for air services to and from this area, and despite the existence of comparatively high intra- and interregional fares, the financial performance of airlines based in this region has been below the world average. The recent downturn in the regional economy has exacerbated the problem for the recently expanded airlines because of the loss of passenger volume and the high-yield characteristic of that traffic. This chapter examines numerous past developments, current trends, and future prospects for the airline industry in this critical area of the world.

Economic, Demographic, and Political Characteristics

The Middle East region encompasses a disparate group of fourteen nations, as shown in figure 4–1 and table 4–1. The United Arab Emirates (UAE) itself

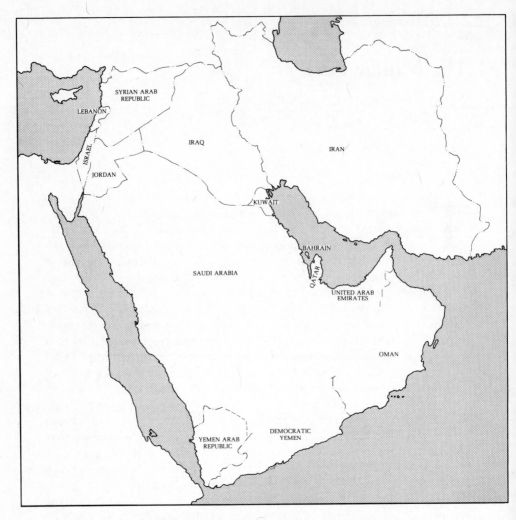

Figure 4–1. The ICAO Middle East Region

is a federation of seven independent Arab nations and is bordered by Qatar, Oman, and Saudi Arabia. Approximately 100 million people (about 2 percent of the world's population) live in the Middle East, which contains about 4 percent of the world's land. About half of the region's total population lives in two countries, Iran and Iraq.

Among the six Gulf states (UAE, Saudi Arabia, Oman, Qatar, Bahrain, and Kuwait) national populations vary from over 10 million in Saudi Arabia to about one-quarter of a million in Qatar. Oil wealth is the largest component of the gross national product for the Gulf states, varying from about 20

Table 4–1
Nations of the ICAO Middle East Region

Nation
Bahrain
Democratic Yemen
Iran
Iraq
Israel
Jordan
Kuwait
Lebanon
Oman
Qatar
Saudi Arabia
Syrian Arab Republic
United Arab Emirates
Abu Dhabi
Ajman
Dubai
Fujairah
Ras al-Khaimah
Sharjah
Umm al-Quwain
Yemen Arab Republic

percent to 60 percent of GNP. The variation in population and oil revenues results in a wide variation in income per capita. During 1983, for example, it is estimated that GNP per capita varied from almost $23,000 in the UAE to about $500 in the People's Democratic Republic of Yemen, clearly the poorest nation in the Middle East. Saudi Arabia, the largest economy in the region, achieved a GNP per capita of just over $12,000. There is also significant variation in the income per capita among the eight non-Gulf states.

The oil-producing countries in the region have distributed the oil wealth, in differing degrees, in the form of government expenditures to improve the socioeconomic conditions of their inhabitants. Governments have made funds available for schools, hospitals, housing, and subsidized utilities, such as water and electricity. Government programs have also included subsidies to airlines.

Since the beginning of this decade, the region's economy has been in a recession. This recession, which has spread out from the Gulf states, has been the result of at least four factors: (1) the decline in the price of oil, (2) the war between Iran and Iraq, (3) the end of the construction boom, and (4) the collapse of an unofficial Kuwaiti stock exchange in 1982. The reduction in the price and production of oil after 1982 has been the primary factor responsible for the recessions in many countries in the region. These recessions have forced curtailments in the levels of most subsidies, thereby raising the cost of living. Not only has the recession-induced loss of subsidized goods and services lowered living standards, but the area's recession has increased unemployment. Many governments are now recognizing the need to restructure their economies so that they become less dependent on oil revenue. The impact of the reductions in oil revenue, as well as the desire to restructure the economy, varies from country to country, depending on factors such as the country's dependence on oil and the development stage of its economy.

The downturn in the economies of the oil-producing countries is also changing the economies of some other countries in the region. Jordan's economy is dependent on foreign aid, the bulk of which comes from the oil-endowed Arab states, and on remittances from Jordanian workers abroad. At the Arab League summit meeting in Baghdad in 1978, Jordan was pledged annual aid in excess of $1 billion for ten years.[1] The fact that Jordan has received less and less aid each year is due to political considerations and the deteriorating condition of the economies in the oil-producing states. Furthermore, the downturn in the oil-based economies has hurt the incomes of Jordanian workers in these countries, which, in turn, has lessened the funds remitted back to Jordan. Coincidentally, an increasing number of Jordanians have been returning home from the oil-producing countries, adding to Jordan's domestic unemployment level. Yemen Arab Republic is another nation whose economy has depended on foreign aid and expatriates' remittances. However, unlike Jordan, oil has recently been discovered in Yemen Arab Republic, a situation that should reduce the nation's dependence on the other two sources of revenue and create more jobs in the domestic economy.

Political tensions are the second factor underlying the worsening state of the economy in this region. Not only has the war between Iran and Iraq brought about a reduction in the amount of oil shipped by these two major producers, it has also led to an increase in insurance costs for ships moving through the Strait of Hormuz. The Gulf war also has increased apprehension among other Middle Eastern countries. Although they are not directly involved, other Middle Eastern governments are devoting a greater proportion of their dwindling revenue bases to building up their own defenses and to supporting the nations involved in the war. In both cases, funds are being spent that could otherwise be used to develop civilian projects. Political considerations in the region have led to a reduction in service offered by some airlines, such as Middle East Airlines (MEA) and the all-cargo carrier, TMA. In addition, political tensions in the Gulf area have affected, to some extent, the operations of Iraqi Airways and Iran Air. MEA and Iran Air used to be the preeminent carriers in this region, but their reduction in operations has led to the rapid emergence of Royal Jordanian (formerly ALIA), Saudia, and

Gulf Air as the region's leading carriers. Air traffic control is another aspect of the air transportation industry affected by the wars in this region. Not only are commercial flights required to fly circuitous routings, but the amount of military traffic has led to serious coordination problems. And, of course, political tensions continue to have an impact on tourism, not just in the Gulf area but in the whole Middle East.

The other two factors contributing to the recession are the end of the construction boom and the collapse of the unofficial Kuwaiti stock exchange. In these government-driven economies, the construction sector depended heavily on redistribution of oil revenues, but in recent years the construction sector of many economies has been suffering in two ways. First, many of the large projects have been completed. Second, other projects are being either delayed or terminated to balance budgets. In the case of the collapse of the Soukh al-Manakh, an unofficial Kuwaiti stock exchange, the impact was not confined to the local financial community in Kuwait. The blow to the confidence in a local financial market led many people to move their funds to financial markets abroad.

In regard to the demographic characteristics of the Middle East, an ICAO study produced in 1982 lists three significant attributes of this region that have influenced the demand for air travel. First, during much of this century, there has been a movement of the population to, from, and within this region. These movements in the population have created communities of interest— and, consequently, a demand for air travel—among a number of other countries. Second, the population density of the Middle East is considered comparable to that of Africa, Latin America, and North America. Third, about two-thirds of the area's population lives in oil-producing countries, in which employment opportunities increased dramatically during the 1970s with increases in the price of oil.[2] The increase in employment opportunities, in turn, had a substantial impact on the demand for air travel.

In addition to the foregoing socioeconomic and demographic characteristics, four other jointly unique characteristics of the region have affected the demand for air travel. First, as a whole, this region has not promoted the development of tourism to the same extent as governments in other areas of the world have. In fact, Saudi Arabia, one of the largest countries in this region, does not allow foreign tourist travel to the kingdom. Recently, some countries (for example, Jordan, Dubai, and Yemen) have taken steps to promote tourism to diversify their economies, which accounts for the emergence of new carriers in some of these countries. Second, although tourist travel may be small or even nonexistent in some countries, there is a significant amount of personal travel, particularly for religious reasons. The Hadj pilgrimage traffic to Saudi Arabia exemplifies this segment of the travel market. All devout Muslims try to make at least one visit to the holy cities of Medina and Mecca. This travel market segment has experienced an enormous growth, not only in total volume but also in the proportion captured by the air mode. In 1973–74, there were 608,000 visits to Saudi Arabia; by 1983–84, the total had risen to 920,000; and in 1985, it was estimated at 1.5 million.[3] The national composition of this traffic has also changed. For example, during 1973–74, the top three originating countries were Pakistan, Iran, and Yemen, in that order. Ten years later, the top three countries were Iran, Egypt, and Pakistan, in that order. Israel is, of course, the other major destination for religious travelers.

Third, the exploitation of the oil industry changed the composition of populations. The extraordinary growth in the economies and the resultant employment opportunities brought in many skilled workers from the West and unskilled workers from the Asia-Pacific region. In 1983, for example, it is estimated that about two-thirds of the labor force in the UAE was non-national. This segment of the population generated substantial demand for air travel. In recent years, there has been a noticeable effort to reduce the percentage of foreign population. Such policy decisions regarding the composition of the population will affect air travel demand in the longer run. Moreover, some of the foreign workers are likely to return to their own countries if their salaries are reduced as a result of the downturn in the economies.

Fourth, the oil boom provided the means for and increased the desire of many Middle East residents to travel. As a result of the influx of petroleum revenues, income per capita in this region rose to levels exceeded only by those in Europe and North America. In addition to the increases in the income per capita, inflation in the economies of the oil-producing countries also had a favorable impact on the demand for air transportation services. In this region, the price of air transportation was insulated from the ravages of inflation, making it appear more attractive in comparison to the costs of other goods and services. Furthermore, many countries in the region committed substantial resources to increasing the level of education of the population. Some analysts claim that higher levels of education, coupled with higher levels of income, create desires in people that cannot be satisfied in the region because of religious beliefs, traditional social constraints, and political conditions.[4] The clash between cultural mores and an interest in forbidden pursuits has become an unusual source of demand for air travel. Since many popular forms of Western entertainment are discouraged in the region, a certain amount of air travel demand has been created by the region's *nouveau riches*, who are traveling to other countries in pursuit of recreational activities.

The Air Transportation System

During the period from the mid-1970s to the mid-1980s, the growth in Middle East passenger traffic was second only to that in the Asia-Pacific region.

And on the basis of this growth in traffic (in particular, the high-yield segment of the market traveling on professional assignments), a number of airlines expanded their operations well beyond the normal growth in the industry. Decreasing oil prices in more recent times have slowed down the growth in passenger travel. Coincidentally, there is now a critical need for major airlines to reassess the scale and nature of their operations, fleet compositions, pricing policies, and travel market targets to be pursued in coming years. The reduction in travel by the professional foreign staff has been particularly detrimental to the airline industry in the region, because it has reduced the volume of travel at the high-yield end of spectrum, which has greatly lowered the average yield.

Table 4–2 presents size data for the ten airlines that (1) are based in this region, (2) are IATA members, and (3) provide scheduled international passenger air services. Combined, this region's airlines performed 3.5 percent of the total world ton-kilometers in all scheduled service in 1985. This share represented an increase of seven-tenths of one percentage point from 1976. In 1985, the shares of international and domestic world scheduled traffic accounted for by this region's airlines were 5.9 and 1.0 percent, respectively.[5] The top three airlines (in terms of total scheduled passenger traffic, measured in passenger-kilometers) are Saudi Arabian Airlines, El Al, and Gulf Air (the multinational airline of Bahrain, Oman, Qatar, and the UAE).

El Al, the largest non-Arab and second largest airline in the Middle East, also achieved significant growth until the end of the 1970s, though not as a

Table 4–2
Middle Eastern Airline Operations, 1985

| Airline | Revenue Passenger-Kilometers (millions) | | | Passengers (000) | | | Employees |
	Int'l	Dom.	Total	Int'l	Dom.	Total	
Alia[a]	3,536	18	3,554	1,220	70	1,290	4,504
El Al	6,502	5	6,507	1,390	18	1,408	3,763
Emirates	40	—	40	24	—	24	125
Gulf Air	4,980	—	4,980	2,870	—	2,870	3,805
Iran Air	2,165	1,806	3,971	928	2,352	3,280	9,988
Kuwait	3,803	—	3,803	1,449	—	1,449	6,240
MEA	930	—	930	501	—	501	4,841
Saudia	10,032	5,426	15,458	3,116	7,679	10,795	25,546
Syrian	929	13	942	442	33	475	3,335
Yemen	560	13	573	318	108	426	1,843

Source: International Air Transport Association (IATA), World Air Transport Statistics, 1985 (Geneva: IATA, June 1986).
[a]Now called Royal Jordanian.

result of increases in oil revenue, as was the case for the other major airlines in the region. During this growth period, unions gained substantial momentum within El Al, partly as a result of management's desire to keep peace. In subsequent years, the airline suffered severe labor problems, resulting in numerous strikes. In 1979, the airline suffered its first loss in fifteen years. It was during a strike by cabin attendants in September 1982 that the government decided to place the airline in provisional receivership, with the goal of reorganizing the company. Operations resumed in January 1983 with new labor contracts, a reduced labor force, and a lower cost structure. It is interesting to note that the airline reduced its labor force by more than 40 percent between 1979 and 1984, while productivity actually increased.[6] Since then, the airline has managed to turn yearly profits despite its singular handicap of operating only six days a week. (The airline does not operate on the Jewish Sabbath.) In recent years, El Al has played a vital role in the development of twin-engine operations over water, using the B-767. El Al was particularly interested in the operation of such an aircraft, since this airline's average length of haul is exceptionally long because of Israel's isolation from its neighbors.

The Regulatory System

As in other regions of the world, air transportation services in the Middle East are provided through bilateral agreements. In the past, the bilateral agreements involving Middle East carriers have tended to be quite conservative. Therefore, like Africa and Latin America, this region as a whole is cautious about increasing liberalization in interregional markets. However, as in Europe, there is a wide variation in attitudes toward liberalization. Gulf states—particularly the UAE and Bahrain, which favor liberalization—are at one extreme; Syria's conservatism is at the other extreme. Saudi Arabia seems to sit in the middle, while Jordan tends to lean toward the liberal attitude of the Gulf states. With respect to intraregional routes, at least in theory, the attitude toward liberalization has been positive for a number of years. For example, the Arab Civil Aviation Council (ACAC) adopted the Marrakech Declaration of 1974, liberalizing traffic rights between Arab countries.[7] Greater liberalization, however, does not mean deregulation or even anything close to it. The policy statement agreed to by the ACAC at its sixteenth session, held in Cairo in 1978, reflects this sentiment very clearly. In accordance with this policy statement, capacity, load factor, and services standards are to be monitored to ensure equity and mutual benefit between bilateral partners.[8] Consequently, most of the scheduled airlines in the Middle East, which are government-owned, are protected by their respective governments with respect to their traffic rights and routes. Moreover, these national airlines have been receiving regular subsidies from their governments. However, recent economic developments and the resultant strains on government budgets have put continuation of such subsidies in jeopardy.

In general, the Middle East region favors a fairly regulated regime, but the policies of individual nations vary significantly, depending on such factors as geography, the potential for foreign trade, and tourism. Moreover, these policies have been subject to change, depending on such factors as the state of the economy and international relations.

Markets

Most of the traffic flow in the Middle East is either regional or international. Domestic traffic accounts for a very small proportion of the total traffic—1 percent, compared to 58 percent in North America, 27.6 percent in Europe, 8.3 percent in the Asia-Pacific region, and 4.1 percent in the Latin America/Caribbean region. Africa is the only other region with such a small percentage of domestic traffic. The size of the domestic market varies, of course, from country to country. For example, in Saudi Arabia, domestic operations account for 35 percent of the total passenger-kilometers but 71 percent of the passengers carried. In Kuwait and the Gulf states, however, there are no domestic air services. There are comprehensive intraregional services connecting all countries, with the exception of Israel.

During the 1970s and early 1980s, the growth in passenger traffic came mostly from the business segment of the market and from the migrant workers of the Asia-Pacific region. Airlines that embarked on major route expansion programs based on trend-line growth projections of these traffic patterns are now facing substantial difficulties. First, the downturn in the regional economy has had a negative impact on both the volume of business travel and the flow of migrant workers. Moreover, the decline in business travel, which is normally high-yield traffic, has had a compounding effect on the overall yields. Second, the downturn in the local oil-based economies is having a negative impact on tourist travel by nationals of these countries.

In examining the major traffic flows from major airports in the region, based on ICAO's on-board statistics, Saudi Arabia is clearly the preeminent country in the region, with three major airports (Dhahran, Jidda, and Riyadh) accounting for a substantial portion of the inter- and intraregional traffic flows. In 1985, Jidda alone served twenty six destinations boarding more than ten passengers per day. Of these twenty six points, ten were in Europe, seven were in the Asia-Pacific region, six were in Africa, and three were in the Middle East. By far the heaviest traffic flows are on the routes to Cairo and Karachi (318,000 and 216,000 passengers per year, respectively, in 1985). These cities are gateways for the rapidly growing pilgrimage traffic. Seven other routes recorded 40,000 or more passengers during 1985. Other important points in the region are Amman, Dubai, and Kuwait. Scheduled services from all three points are available to North America, Europe, Africa, and the Asia-Pacific region.

Because of its geographic location, the Middle East region has traditionally played a vital role in the movement of traffic between Europe and the Asia-Pacific region. Historically, Beirut, Bahrain, and Tehran were important transit points in the east–west traffic flow. Prior to 1975, Beirut was an important commercial and financial center in the Middle East because of its free-market philosophy, its geographic location, and its trade in transit traffic. At one point, Pan Am's eastbound and westbound round-the-world flights used to stop at Beirut. The political and religious disturbances since then have diminished Beirut's prominent position as the center of activity in the Middle East.

Because of the political situation, a desire to capture a greater share of the total transit traffic, and the route structure and pricing policies of their respective airlines, Amman, Bahrain, Dubai, and Kuwait have become more prominent international hubs, whereas Beirut and Tehran now account for a much smaller share of the total east–west transit traffic. Accordingly, these countries' flag carriers have become the region's leading airlines. Bahrain, in particular, is emerging as an air transportation center among the Gulf states. Its international airport is already the center of aviation in the Gulf area. And the causeway linking Bahrain with Saudi Arabia could increase transborder travel and raise the activity of commercial aviation at Bahrain's airport even more.

In the past, the Middle East's location as a convenient midpoint on intercontinental routes, coupled with the limited range and capacity characteristics of previous generations of aircraft, provided an opportunity for a number of carriers based in this region to take advantage of sixth-freedom traffic. For example, table 4–3 shows the published *intraline* connections at three points in the Middle East between flights from the Asia-Pacific region and other regions in the world during April 1987. Royal Jordanian's flight from Kuala Lumpur to Amman connects with flights from Amman to points in North America, Europe, and Africa. Kuwait Airways' flights from Bombay to Kuwait connect with this airline's flights to North America, Europe, Africa, and points within the Middle East. Similarly, Gulf Air's flights from Bangkok to Bahrain connect with this airline's flights to other regions. Airlines transporting sixth-freedom passenger traffic tend to discount fares in order to attract such traffic. The amount of discount depends on such factors as the availability and quality of alternative service and the quality of intraline connections offered by the sixth-freedom carrier. Intraline connections, with either lengthy transit times at the intermediate airport or indirect routings, tend to be heavily discounted. It is ironic that Saudi Arabia, the largest carrier in the region, is unable to take advantage of the sixth-freedom traffic, partly because of the prohibitive visa requirements of the Saudi government.

Table 4–3
Intraline Connections at Three Airports in the Middle East

Royal Jordanian[a] via Amman	Kuwait Airways via Kuwait	Gulf Air via Bahrain
Kuala Lumpur to:	Bombay to:	Bangkok to:
Amsterdam	Amsterdam	Athens
Brussels	Athens	Frankfurt
Geneva	Frankfurt	Larnaca
London	Geneva	London
Madrid	London	Paris
Paris	Madrid	Amman
Rome	Paris	Cairo
Vienna	Rome	Dharan
New York	Damascus	Jidda
Tripoli	Dharan	Istanbul
	Istanbul	Kuwait
	Jidda	Riyadh
	Cairo	
	Casablanca	
	Tripoli	
	Tunis	

Source: ABC International, *ABC World Airways Guide* (Dunstable, U.K.: ABC International, April 1987).
[a]Formerly Alia.

Competition among airlines to direct sixth-freedom traffic over their own countries has increased to the point that there is now competition even among the countries that own their own multinational airlines, led by Gulf Air. Initially, Bahrain began to compete for transit traffic with UAE states (for example, Dubai and Sharjah). Subsequently, the desire of some individual Gulf states to lure sixth-freedom traffic became so intense that Dubai established its own airline (Emirates) to compete with its multinational airline, Gulf Air.

In the past ten years, there has been a massive investment in airports in the Middle East, particularly in the Gulf states and in Saudi Arabia. In the Gulf states, the anticipated growth in traffic between Europe and the Far East provided the incentive to commit to this investment. A large percentage of this traffic is, in fact, being handled through the airports in the Gulf states. However, the existence of a large number of airports in the Gulf states has produced overcapacity in the system. For example, there are now major airports in Abu Dhabi, Dubai, Ras al-Khaimah, and Sharjah, all within a distance of about 150 to 200 miles. Obviously, the total airport capacity in the

UAE alone far exceeds the capacity required to fulfill the needs of the local population, including tourists and visitors. Consequently, there is fierce competition among the surrounding airports to attract traffic, particularly long-haul airlines. This competition has led to an open-skies policy on the part of some countries, resulting in comparatively low landing and ground handling fees for airlines and extremely attractive duty-free shopping facilities for passengers.

Although Gulf Air had been well positioned to take advantage of emerging opportunities, politics and nationalism are now presenting significant challenges for the airline. Gulf Air has been the flag carrier of Bahrain, Oman, Qatar, and the UAE. However, from the viewpoint of ownership, only one member of the UAE (Abu Dhabi) is a shareholder. In recent years, another member of the UAE (Dubai) not only has been promoting procompetitive policies and offering economic incentives to foreign airlines to operate through its international airports but has also financed the development of another airline to compete with Gulf Air. Moreover, the competitive fight among the countries that have an interest in Gulf Air has weakened the bargaining position for traffic rights for Gulf Air.

Fares

In theory, both the IATA and the Arab Air Carriers Organization (AACO) play an active role in the coordination of passenger fares for scheduled services involving the Middle East region. Membership in the AACO allows airlines based in this region to discuss various tariff proposals before they are presented at the larger IATA traffic conferences. Some members of the AACO also coordinate their tariff activities with the African Airlines Association (AFRAA) prior to the IATA meetings. In reality, however, reaching agreement through the IATA framework has often been a difficult process for at least three reasons: (1) local carriers' desire to capitalize on Middle East transit traffic, (2) overcapacity, and (3) the intricacies of fares between Europe and Israel and fares between the Middle East and Africa. As a result, the IATA's tariff-coordinating power has eroded considerably, and there is widespread discounting. Under normal circumstances, fares are set through bilateral channels in the event of a breakdown in the IATA tariff-coordinating process. However, in the Middle East, overcapacity and the intense rivalry among nations, particularly in the Gulf area, have led to extensive discounting of even the bilaterally agreed fares. Actual fares typically run 50 percent below the IATA-recommended fares. A number of carriers are attempting to attract business travelers with discount fares. Attempts by the Arab Air Carriers Organization and the Gulf Co-operation States have not been successful in stopping unauthorized discounting.[9] The growing importance of pilgrimage traffic will also exert a downward force on fares.

Table 4–4 presents a comparison of the published average normal economy fares for two route groups for various distance groups.[10] In all cases, the

Table 4–4

Comparison of Average Normal Economy Fares per Kilometer in the Middle East, September 1985

Route Group	Cents/Kilometer by Distance (km)				
	200	*500*	*1,000*	*2,000*	*4,000*
Middle East	31.8	25.5	20.4	16.3	—
Europe–Middle East	—	—	23.0	19.3	16.2
Int'l total—world	28.7	23.6	19.4	16.0	13.2
Middle East as percentage of world	111	108	105	102	—
Europe–Middle East as percentage of world	—	—	119	121	123

Source: International Civil Aviation Organization (ICAO), *Survey of International Air Transport Fares and Rates, September 1985* (Montreal: ICAO, June 1986), 16.

officially quoted normal economy fares were higher than the world average by between 2 and 23 percent. For the local Middle East data, the ICAO's sample consisted of 306 city pairs among the countries in the region and also included Cyprus. The majority of the city pairs (125, or 40.8 percent) fell in the 1,000–1,999 km distance group. For this group, normal economy fares were only 5 percent higher than the world average. For the Europe–Middle East route group, the sample consisted of 682 city pairs, the majority of which (374, or 54.8 percent) fell in the 2,000–3,999 km distance group. For this group, normal economy fares were 21 percent higher than the world average. It is important to keep in mind, however, that all airlines offer a variety of official discount fares and that many offer a broad spectrum of under-the-table discounts, with the distribution of traffic by fare category varying from airline to airline.

The ICAO conducted a survey in 1980 to examine the extent of discount fares available to the public. The general conclusion to be drawn from these data is that most Middle East passengers have had access to discount fares either through normal distribution sources or by spurious means. The lower discount fares continue to exist, although the percentage of discount available differs from airline to airline, depending on the socioeconomic characteristics of the market and the pricing policies of individual airlines. Table 4–5 shows the discounts from the normal fare available on a sample of ten routes between the Middle East and Europe and within the Middle East.

Financial Performance

Although airlines based in the Middle East have experienced rapid growth in traffic during the past fifteen years, their financial performance has been be-

Table 4–5
Available Discounts from Normal Fares in the Middle East, September 1985

City Pair (originating city first)	Flight Distance (km)	Normal Economy (U.S.$)	Individual Fares					Group Fares	
			First Class	Excursion	PEX	Individual Inclusive Tour	Other[a]	Group Inclusive Tour	Group Other Than Inclusive Tour[b]
			(as a percentage of normal economy fare)						
London–Abu Dhabi	5,496	1,302	205	97	–	–	–	–	–
Dubai–Brussels	5,147	1,836	144	68	–	–	–	–	–
Zurich–Dhahran	4,315	1,463	143	67	–	–	–	–	–
Jidda–Algiers	3,849	1,192	137	68	–	–	–	47	–
Amsterdam–Tel Aviv	3,314	1,059	146	49–59	34	–	–	33	46
Cairo–Frankfurt	2,921	989	145	67	–	–	–	–	–
Warsaw–Damascus	2,464	816	147	68	–	–	–	–	–
Tehran–Athens	2,462	844	139	75	–	–	–	–	–
Sofia–Baghdad	2,099	1,065	139	68	–	–	–	–	–
Amman–Istanbul	1,188	447	129	67	–	–	–	–	–

Source: International Civil Aviation Organization (ICAO), *Survey of International Air Transport Fares and Rates, September 1985* (Montreal: ICAO, June 1986), 67.

[a]Special fares existed for ships' crews, families, students and youths (and also for pilgrims to Jidda). These fares are at levels between 25 and 55 percent below the level of the applicable normal economy fare.

[b]Special fares were available throughout this route group for ships' crews at 35 percent below the level of the normal economy fare.

low the world average. This result can be explained by the fact that although both the growth in traffic and the level of revenue yield were above the world average, both the increase in unit operating costs and the level of load factor were below the world average. For example, between 1970 and 1979, six airlines (Royal Jordanian, El Al, Kuwait, MEA, Saudia, and TMA), representing 77 percent of the region's total scheduled traffic, experienced an average increase in revenue of 26.9 percent per year, while costs increased at a rate of 27.2 percent per year. The region's aggregate load factor—measured by the ratio of revenue ton-kilometers (RTK) to available ton-kilometers (ATK)—was 4.6 percentage points above the world average in 1970, but deteriorated to 7.7 percentage points below the world average in 1979.[11] This trend seems to have continued during the 1980s. For example, during 1985, average yield remained higher than world average for routes within the Middle East and between Europe and Middle East, while load factors remained below world average (see table 4–6). According to the ICAO analysis for the period between 1970 and 1979, three categories of costs were responsible for the unfavorable financial results: depreciation and amortization; general and administrative; and ticketing, sales, and promotion.[12] Higher than world average costs in these three categories offset the lower than average costs in some other categories, particularly fuel.

As in other regions, with the exception of the United States, some carriers are more profit-oriented than others. Those airlines whose governments view them as providers of public service generally tend to be more handicapped. A case in point would be an airline such as Saudia, which maintains relatively low fares for domestic services. Conversely, Royal Jordanian is an example of an airline with market orientation.

Part of the past problem resulted from an enormous expansion of operations, leading to equally enormous investment requirements and heightened financial leverage. Unfortunately, significant financial investments will still be required to replace the older airplanes of the B-707/DC-8 vintage (about 20 percentage of the fleet at the beginning of 1987). And unless the financial performance improves significantly, the burden will have to be borne by the governments, either directly or indirectly through guarantees. Governments, however, having experienced downturns in their economies as a result of reductions in oil revenues, are placing more pressure on their airlines to improve their financial performance. Operating subsidies are being reduced and airlines are being pressured to become more efficient.

The airlines will not be able to boost revenues by raising their fares. Within the Middle East, passenger fares are already high relative to normal economy world averages, and the proportion of discount traffic and the level of those discounts will not change because of overcapacity and the fierce rivalries among nations. Therefore, it seems that the airlines based in this region will be forced either to reduce their costs or to increase revenue in

Table 4–6
Load Factors in Scheduled Service, Middle East, 1985
(percentages)

Route Area	RPK/ASK	RTK/ATK
Europe–Middle East	58.4	53.2
Middle East–Far East	61.7	54.5
Africa–Middle East	55.2	48.6
Within Middle East	54.4	47.0
Total IATA international	64.5	60.1

Source: International Air Transport Association (IATA), *World Air Transport Statistics, 1985* (Geneva: IATA, June 1986).
RPK = revenue passenger-kilometers; ASK = available seat-kilometers; RTK = revenue ton-kilometers; ATK = available ton-kilometers.

ways other than by increasing fares, or both. In the area of cost reductions, the more aggressive airlines are taking on a strategic orientation in which the emphasis is on examining cost structures more than costs levels. Other airlines could end up either scaling down their operations or, to a limited extent (much more limited than in other regions of the world), merging with other airlines or providing joint operations. In the areas of revenue increases, more emphasis is being placed on yield management and on a change in operations for some carriers.

Future Prospects

As in the past, the fortunes of carriers based in the Middle East will largely be determined by the price of oil and regional events in the political arena. Regrettably, there is no way reasonably to predict the future with respect to either variable. The general trend in the oil-producing countries is to diversify their economies by developing ancillary industries to provide some protection against the effects of volatile oil revenues. Since the severity of the recession has not been the same in all countries—because different countries are at different stages of development—the need to adjust to the new conditions varies from country to country. Nonetheless, there are not too many options for starting different types of industries and businesses in countries whose primary natural resources are oil and gas. Everything else, including materials and labor, has to be imported. Moreover, this region's cultural heritage is not receptive to commercial emigration from Western nations. Investment in international markets is the other option. Although such an option may provide a hedge against uncertainties of the oil market, it does not produce employment opportunities for the national work force or any significant demand for air travel.

The structure and growth of Middle Eastern airlines will continue to be closely tied to petroleum revenues for at least three reasons. First, as was just shown, the regional economy—and hence air transportation demand—will rely heavily on the oil industry. Second, government subsidies to airlines will rise and fall in concert with petroleum receipts. Third, if the price of oil does not increase significantly in the near future, the inevitable reductions in government-supported projects and subsidies may lead to higher costs of living, higher unemployment, and, in some cases, structural changes in the economy, such as the introduction of income taxes. Of course, the reverse scenario would unfold with an upturn in Middle East oil production. These types of changes do not imply that the economies of the Gulf area will decline significantly; rather, they imply that the growth may follow a more normal rate compared to the phenomenal growth achieved since 1973. Similarly, the demand for air travel will not necessarily decline; rather, the growth will follow rates comparable to those in other regions of the world.

One development that could have a major impact on the market structure of the airline industry in this region is a decision by Saudi Arabia to relax control of its market. Given the size and economic importance of this country, and given the fact that Saudia is already the largest national airline in the region, the airline could take on a new dimension in its growth if the market becomes more relaxed. Even if the government continues its restrictive policy on tourism, some relaxation with respect to visa requirements could provide Saudia the option to participate in sixth-freedom traffic.

An ongoing problem that will plague these airlines even if competition remains controlled is excess capacity as a result of flights between Europe and the Asia-Pacific region passing through the Middle East. This overcapacity, coupled with various countries' desire to direct the through-flights via their nations, has prompted them to expand frequency and has kept pressure on yields. In addition, aggressive new airlines, such as Emirates, will no doubt aggravate the overcapacity problem. So far, the growth of Emirates has been contained; for example, this airlines has not been able to get route rights to Saudi Arabia or Kuwait. However, it is only a question of time.

Although a number of airlines in the Asia-Pacific region have increased their frequency through the region, advancements in airplane technology will slow the growth of such additions to capacity. New-generation airplanes are now capable of flying nonstop between Europe and the Far East. Their ca-

pacity, range, and economic performance could eliminate the need for intermediate stops in the Middle East. This development could lead the airlines in
the Middle East to take one of two courses. As the number of intercontinental
nonstop flights increases, there could be a corresponding decline in overcapacity in the Middle East markets if the airlines based in this region reduce
their capacity to a level needed for third- and fourth-freedom traffic rather
than fifth-freedom traffic. The resultant decline in overcapacity could reduce
the need to undercut fares. Alternatively, if the airlines decide not to reduce
their capacity, they will most likely resort to competitive pricing to attract
traffic, and the average yield would deteriorate even further. Moreover, the
Middle Eastern airlines may feel compelled to offer bigger discounts to divert
Europe–Far East traffic that would otherwise fly nonstop. Unfortunately, the
strategies appear to be heading in the direction of increasing capacity. In the
final analysis, the key to future revenue growth will be cost-effective yield
management.

The change in economic conditions has already slowed down the growth
in traffic experienced by the carriers in the region. To the extent that growth
does occur over and above that attributable to changes in population and
national income, it will come from the expanded services of such carriers as
Royal Jordanian, Gulf Air, and Saudia. For services to Europe, the emphasis
is likely to be on frequency. For interregional services, the emphasis is likely
to be on new routes. For example, Gulf Air could expand its services to Africa
and Royal Jordanian could expand its services to South America.

Unlike other regions, the Middle East is not likely to experience airline
consolidation, given the importance of national prestige. Saudia is already a
large airline by world standards, and Royal Jordanian, Gulf Air, and Kuwait
Airways are on their way to becoming large carriers. If a consolidation were
to occur between Saudia and another airline—such as Gulf Air or Kuwait
Airways, or both—it would produce a megacarrier well positioned to compete with its counterparts in other regions. As for the smaller airlines, not
only will they survive with the support of their governments, but some could
actually become aggressive competitors. Examples include the newly formed
Emirates, based in Dubai and Yemenia (North Yemen). Both the larger and
the smaller airlines have benefited from their governments' policies to promote tourism. The other smaller, government-protected airlines that do survive could, however, be forced to scale down their operations to the point
that they simply meet the needs of the third- and fourth-freedom traffic and
serve other routes that are in the national interest of their governments. Furthermore, if the recession is worse than anticipated and the Middle East governments move to lessen financial ties with their national airlines, even the
largest carriers may be forced to take drastic actions, as exemplified by the
massive cuts by El Al in this region and British Airways in Europe.

Notes

1. Europa, *The Europa Year Book 1986* (London: Europa Publications, 1986), 1525–26.

2. International Civil Aviation Organization (ICAO), *Middle East: International Air Passenger and Freight Transport* (Montreal: ICAO, January 1982).

3. *Europa Year Book 1986*, 2251.

4. "Gulf Cooperation Council Survey," *The Economist*, 8 February 1986, 5–6.

5. International Civil Aviation Organization (ICAO), *Bulletin* (Montreal: ICAO, June 1986), 25.

6. Nachman L. Klieman, "El Al Israel Airlines," in *Airfinance Annual* (London: Airfinance Journal, 1985–86), 136.

7. ICAO, *Middle East*, 36.

8. Ibid., 37.

9. David Woolley, "Arab Air Transport: The Problems of Maturity," *Interavia*, July 1985, 755–60.

10. International Civil Aviation Organization (ICAO), *Survey of International Air Transport Fares and Rates, September 1985* (Montreal: ICAO, June 1986).

11. ICAO, *Middle East*, 101–2.

12. Ibid., 105.

5
Africa

C ivil aviation is an integral component of national defense and a facilitator of national political, social, and economic policies. A sound national airline can be a valuable resource for any developing country. As a result, developing nations claim that they cannot depend on services provided by foreign airlines over which they may have no control. However, an unsuccessful national airline not only is a lost opportunity but is a real liability for a country already saddled with a crippling debt burden, falling commodity prices, dwindling export revenues, an impoverished population, an almost nonexistent industrial base, stagnating agricultural output, and spiraling costs. Many governments in Africa that operate national airlines are faced with monumental challenges: first, how to derive the advantages that a national airline can provide without placing a huge financial burden on the state and, second, what changes, if any, to make in the operating environment to position their airlines to overcome operational obstacles unique to the African air transportation market. This chapter examines trends in and prospects for the African airline industry. Since the operations of many airlines based in this region are handicapped by numerous institutional barriers, a section of the chapter is devoted to barriers to progress.

Economic, Demographic, and Political Characteristics

Geographically, Africa is the second largest continent in the world, and it is the third largest in population. This region contains fifty-two nations and two dependent territories of extraregional nations, as shown in figure 5–1. Table 5–1 groups these nations and territories into the five subregions defined by the ICAO. Africa accounts for about 20 percent of the world's land, about 10 percent of the world's population, but less than 5 percent of the world's gross national product. The African continent is extremely diverse, spanning a broad range of ethnic groupings, political ideologies, vegetation, topogra-

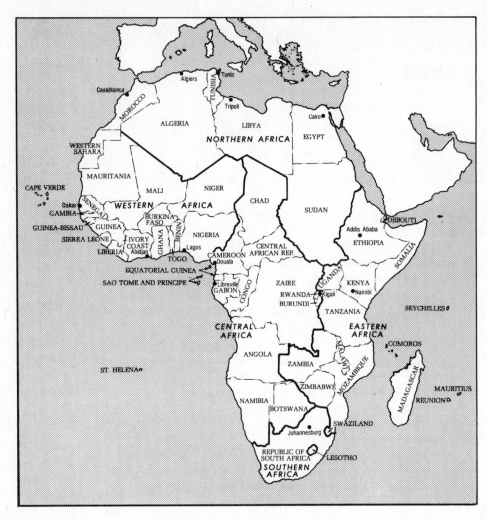

Figure 5–1. The ICAO Africa Region

phy, and climate. Despite this diversity, it is possible to make the following generalizations: (1) national economies are underdeveloped and overly dependent on external trade, investment, and foreign aid; (2) population growth continually offsets advances in socioeconomic areas; and (3) most countries are constrained by low literacy rates.

The GNP per capita in sub-Sahara Africa increased at an average annual rate of 1.3 percent in real terms between 1960 and 1970, but between 1970 and 1980 it grew only 0.7 percent annually. Excluding Nigeria, GNP per capita did not increase at all during the 1970s; and during the early 1980s, the real output actually declined.[1] With the exception of South Africa, most

Table 5–1
Nations and Dependent Territories of the ICAO Africa Region

Northern Africa
ICAO Contracting States
Algeria
Egypt
Libyan Arab Jamahiriya
Morocco
Sudan
Tunisia

Western Africa
ICAO Contracting States
Benin
Cape Verde
Gambia
Ghana
Guinea
Guinea-Bissau
Ivory Coast
Liberia
Mali
Mauritania
Niger
Nigeria
Senegal
Sierra Leone
Togo
Upper Volta (Burkina Faso)

Central Africa
ICAO Contracting States
Angola
Burundi
Central African Republic
Chad
Congo
Equatorial Guinea
Gabon

Rwanda
Sao Tome and Principe
United Republic of Cameroon
Zaire

ICAO Noncontracting State
Namibia

Dependent Territory
St. Helena (U.K.)

Eastern Africa
ICAO Contracting States
Botswana
Djibouti
Ethiopia
Kenya
Lesotho
Madagascar
Malawi
Mauritius
Mozambique
Somalia
Seychelles
Swaziland
Uganda
United Republic of Tanzania
Zambia
Zimbabwe

ICAO Noncontracting State
Comoros

Dependent Territory
Reunion (France)

Southern Africa
ICAO Contracting State
South Africa

Source: International Civil Aviation Organization (ICAO), *International Air Passenger and Freight Transport: Africa* (Montreal: ICAO, March 1985), 109.

African nations are considered developing economies, with average annual GNPs per capita of less than $1,000. This level of personal income is clearly too low to allow discretionary travel by the general public. In many parts of Africa, well over half of the income per capita must be committed to food, and the composition of consumer demand is almost entirely based on the consumption of luxury items by the 20 percent of the population that accumulates over two-thirds of the national income. The other 80 percent of the population is either earning little more than subsistence wages or providing for most of its needs by semisubsistence farming.[2]

Nevertheless, there is significant variation in economic conditions across the continent. For instance, countries such as Chad, Ethiopia, Mali, Burkina Faso, and Zaire have incomes per capita of about $200. At the other end of the economic spectrum, Libyan Arab Jamahiriya's GNP per capita approaches $10,000, a level comparable to that in most countries in Western Europe. Other countries with relatively high incomes per capita are Reunion (France), Gabon, South Africa, Algeria, Namibia, and Seychelles. However, among this latter group of countries, high incomes per capita are simply the result of small populations. Consequently, only five of the fifty four countries (South Africa, Nigeria, Algeria, Libyan Arab Jamahiriya, and Morocco) account for two-thirds of Africa's total GNP.[3]

Although most of the countries in the western, eastern, and central subregions of Africa are heavily dependent on the agricultural sector, a modest industrial base does exist in the northern and southern subregions. Just five countries (Algeria, Egypt, Morocco, Nigeria, and South Africa) account for about 80 percent of Africa's total industrial production. Some industrial progress (measured as an increasing share of GNP) has been made over the past two decades, although the level remains below that of other regions, such as Asia and Latin America. In the agricultural sector, there has been a decrease in the production of food, resulting from (1) the large-scale migration of rural populations into towns, (2) a broad range of economic distortions imposed on the agricultural sector by the governments, and (3) the prolonged drought in a number of sub-Saharan countries.

The African nations account for less than 3 percent of total world exports, most of which are intercontinental rather than intra-Africa. This figure, small as it is, has been declining since the beginning of this decade. Mining accounts for about half of the region's total value exports. The top mineral-exporting countries are Algeria, Libya, Nigeria, South Africa, and Zambia. The decline in exports has also been accompanied by a decline in imports, resulting in a reduction in the total volume of trade. The collapse of the oil market has been a mixed blessing for the African continent. It has benefited many sub-Saharan nations that import oil, but the oil-producing nations—such as Congo, Gabon, and Nigeria—have suffered an economic fate similar to that of the nations of the Middle East.

The tourism industry is an integral component of the national economy in a number of countries in Africa, including Algeria, Egypt, Kenya, Mauritius, Morocco, Seychelles, and Tunisia. The majority of the tourists arrive from Western Europe, and they use scheduled services for the most part.

In the past, many countries have been dependent on foreign aid and loans. However, the financial plight of many countries has become so serious that international lending agencies are attaching stringent demands for economic policy reforms as loan criteria. Some of these criteria, such as the dissolution of inefficient state enterprises and the privatization of those enterprises that could be made viable, could affect the airline industry. Many governments are, of course, resisting the imposition of these loan conditions. However, given the performance of many countries with respect to their indebtedness, it is likely that they will be compelled to accept these conditions. At the end of 1985, the total debt of sub-Saharan Africa was estimated to be approaching $100 billion.[4] Moreover, the rising debt balance is severely straining the debtor nations' ability to service such obligations.

It is also quite difficult to attract outside investment because of the unstable political climate, the generally poor economic environment, and the stringent exchange controls imposed by some African countries. For example, exchange controls have led to severe currency remittance difficulties and to cash flow problems for international airlines, resulting in withdrawal of some services. One reason Pan American reduced its service to Africa was the airline's inability to transfer funds out of the countries it served. Now Pan American's service is limited to Nairobi, Kenya. It is ironic that even the African airlines are faced with the problem of blocked revenues, which further aggravates an already poor financial performance.[5]

The unstable political climate is a function of this region's numerous ethnic groups, artificial boundaries, and regionally entrenched interests. The rivalries and territorial disputes have produced instability in many parts of the continent and are a major drain on Africa's development. Besides creating an unstable political environment, these political confrontations have increased the continent's military spending, have contributed to the continent's economic decline, and have forced massive movements in population, dramatized by the expulsion of up to 2 million migrants from Nigeria in early 1983.[6]

The Air Transportation System

During the past two decades, the airline industry in Africa has achieved growth rates above the world average. Despite this above-average growth, the total volume of traffic remains small. Europe, with less than half the population of Africa, generates ten times more aviation activity. At present, the output of some individual airlines in Europe and North America exceeds the combined total output of all airlines in Africa.

Many of the problems confronting the African national airlines can be associated with lower load factors and lower utilization, which, in turn, are a function of the number of carriers trying to operate in the small African market. About seventy five international airlines are based in Africa, employing almost 100,000 people. More than half of these airlines offer scheduled service, and about one-fourth are all-cargo carriers. In addition, Africa is served by about fifty outside airlines, about half of them from Europe. Airlines based in Africa are very small by world standards. Even the largest airline, South African Airways, is smaller than all major airlines in the United States, most of the national flag carriers in Europe, Saudia in the Middle East, and about half a dozen carriers based in the Asia-Pacific region. Table 5–2 presents size data for the top fifteen airlines based in Africa. In 1985, these fifteen airlines combined produced fewer passenger-kilometers in total scheduled service than each of the top seven members of IATA. The combined output of the top fifteen airlines in Africa was less than half the output of each of the two largest airlines in the United States (American and United) and was comparable to the output of a single airline the size of Air France.

In addition to the scheduled airlines, there are about two dozen small airlines offering nonscheduled services. There are three common character-

Table 5–2
The Top Fifteen African Airlines with International Scheduled Service, 1985

Airline	Passenger-Kilometers (millions)		Passengers (000)		Employees
	Int'l	Total	Int'l	Total	
South African A/W	5,600	8,683	712	4,207	11,687
Egyptair	4,002	4,427	1,757	2,786	11,599
Air Algerie	2,797	2,797	2,246	2,246	7,060
Air Afrique	2,321	2,321	735	735	5,795[a]
Royal Air Maroc	2,099	2,122	1,038	1,114	4,103
Nigeria A/W[a]	1,100	2,006	400	1,946	9,036
Libyan Arab A/L	1,034	1,672	601	1,579	4,880
Tunis Air	1,457	1,499	1,154	1,282	4,633
Ethiopian A/L	913	1,016	244	471	3,285
Kenya A/W	707	770	225	376	2,753
Air Zimbabwe	559	661	189	453	1,748
Zambia A/W	620	654	140	254	1,608
Air Mauritius	638	642	176	183	600
Air Gabon	425	516	131	456	1,567
Air Zaire	240	355	54	151	2,521

Sources: International Civil Aviation Organization (ICAO), *Civil Aviation Statistics of the World* (Montreal: ICAO, August, 1986); and International Air Transport Association (IATA), *World Air Transport Statistics, 1985* (Geneva: IATA, June 1986).
[a]1984 data.

istics of the African nonscheduled airline industry. First, the turnover in this segment of the industry is very high. For example, in 1978 and 1983, fifteen and twenty-two airlines, respectively, were offering charter service in Africa. Only three of these airlines were operating in both years.[7] Second, most of the nonscheduled airlines transport freight traffic, such as agricultural products, to Europe. Third, most of the long-haul nonscheduled airlines operate the older B-707/DC-8 type of airplanes. In the past, these airlines were able to justify low utilization of their fleets because of the low acquisition costs of these airplanes. The situation undoubtedly will change in the future, when these airplanes are not allowed to operate to European capitals because of noise regulations that apply to older airplanes.

In 1985, the commercial fleet operated by Africa's top fifteen airlines offering scheduled domestic and international service totaled 279 (see table 5–3). Wide-body airplanes made up less than one-fourth of the fleet. The most commonly operated types were the B-737 (sixty-two), the B-707 (forty three), and the B-727 (forty). It should be noted that *at least* forty three air-

Table 5–3
The Top Fifteen African Airlines and Their Fleets, 1985

Airline	B-747	DC-10	A-300/ B-767	DC-8/ B-720/ B-707	B-727	DC-9/ B-737	Other	Total
South African A/W	15	—	8	—	—	17	—	40
Egyptair	1[a]	—	11	6	—	6	3	27
Air Algerie	—	—	2	4	9	9	1	25
Air Afrique	1	3	3	2	—	—	—	9
Royal Air Maroc	2	—	—	2	8	6	—	18
Nigeria A/W[b]	2	2	4	3	2	10	9	32
Libyan Arab A/L	—	—	—	3	10	—	18	31
Tunis Air	—	—	1	—	8	6[a]	—	15
Ethiopian A/L	—	—	2	6	3	—	17	28
Kenya A/W	—	1[a]	1[a]	5[a]	—	1	2	10
Air Zimbabwe	—	—	—	5	—	1[a]	6	12
Zambia A/W	—	1	—	3	—	1	2	7
Air Mauritius	1[a]	—	—	2	—	1[a]	3[a]	7
Air Gabon	1	—	—	—	—	1	6	8
Air Zaire	—	1	—	2	—	3	4	10
Total	23	8	32	43	40	62	71	279

Sources: International Civil Aviation Organization (ICAO), *Civil Aviation Statistics of the World* (Montreal: ICAO, August, 1986); and International Air Transport Association (IATA), *World Air Transport Statistics, 1985* (Geneva: IATA, June 1986).
[a]Some or all airplanes leased.
[b]1983 data.

planes (15 percent) in the fleets of the top airlines in the region will not meet the noise requirements contained in Annex 16 to the Chicago Convention. These standards become effective worldwide on January 1, 1988. The 15 percent figure includes only the B-707/DC-8 type of airplanes. The percentage becomes much higher when pre-1974 models of B-727s, B-737s and DC-9s are taken into consideration. A much higher percentage of the fleets of the remaining airlines, particularly charter airlines, will be affected. It is estimated that almost one-third of the African airlines' fleets may not meet pending noise requirements.

The Regulatory System

Of the fifty-six participants at the Chicago Conference in 1944, four were from Africa. Now there are more than 150 member nations in the ICAO, and one-third are from Africa. Governments in this area often make reference to the Chicago Convention of 1944, during which the signatory governments agreed to the principles of "equality of opportunity." Since then, the bilateral regulatory system and the multilateral fare-setting mechanism have allowed African airlines an equal opportunity to participate in the international air transport system. Furthermore, individual nations and airlines have a framework for pursuing national policy objectives. For example, through a bilateral agreement, an airline can negotiate an adequate market share, and the IATA multilateral fare-setting mechanism offers the promise of protection with respect to tariffs.

It is not surprising, then, that most African governments are violently opposed to an unregulated regime encompassing multiple designation, free capacity, and pricing formulas based on the costs of the most efficient carrier. These nations do not have the luxury of multiple airlines that would offer competitive service or would be ready to take over abandoned markets if a competing airline went bankrupt. Furthermore, the African countries' airline investment is made at the expense of other desirable public expenditures, not to provide a return on investment commensurate with the risks. In such a context, this region's nations and airlines were extremely concerned when the United States began to promote its open-skies policy and again when the IATA adopted its two-tier membership system.

African airlines argue that the close relationship between civil aviation and national public interests dictates that the future of civil aviation cannot be left to the forces of the marketplace. They contend not only that regulatory intervention is justified but that the financial benefits of a national airline cannot be measured strictly by the operating results of the airline. Any cost-benefit analysis of airline service must also measure the indirect contributions to the economy and to the national defense, and it must take into account the need to coordinate air transportation activities with the other components of the region's underdeveloped transportation network.[8]

Three other considerations relate directly to the market for air transportation in this region and the motivation for continued imposition of strict government control. First, the African governments claim that uncontrolled competition is not appropriate for their region because the market is price-inelastic. Accordingly, any reductions in airline fares that might result from the elimination of regulatory controls would not necessarily lead to significant increases in the demand for air transportation. Second, governments claim that their airlines generally operate in third- and fourth-freedom markets only, resulting in limited opportunities for the national airlines. Third, market densities are so low that they cannot support even one airline, let alone two or three.

Fare-setting and capacity controls traditionally have benefited the airlines in this region in terms of maintaining high yields on international flights with lower load factors. Lower load factors are primarily the result of low traffic densities. Of course, high fares also contribute to low load factors, but the African markets are so thin and so price-inelastic that lower fares would not generate sufficient traffic to offset the revenue loss associated with lower fares. To protect their national airlines, African governments have approved fares above levels justified from a purely economic perspective. However, the situation is changing. No longer is it feasible for governments to decide on the size and nature of operations of their national carrier without giving much consideration to the needs and requirements of the marketplace. Governments must now face the reality of competitiveness, at least in the long-haul markets. The African Air Traffic Conference (AFRATC) was proposed in 1979 as a vehicle to support and promote the interest of this region when changes began to be introduced in the IATA traffic conference machinery.

All of the major airlines in Africa are government-owned and government-controlled. One airline, Air Afrique, is multinational; it is owned by ten French-speaking African nations and the French airline UTA. An ICAO study succinctly sums up the theory behind the airline industry in Africa: "African States usually look on their national airline as an essential instrument of international trade and communications and an integral part of the national economic and social development process."[9] Government ownership and control place significant obligations and constraints on the national airline with respect to routes, management functions, and the selection of airplanes. As a result, commercial considerations very often end up taking a back seat to political considerations. On the other hand, government ownership also entails financial and operational support for the national airline.

Since almost all governments in Africa hold similarly protective views about their national airlines, the entire industry is tightly regulated. For example, more than half of the bilateral agreements contain predetermination capacity clauses. Fifth-freedom traffic rights are granted on a very limited basis, and when they are granted, they are usually accompanied by operational restrictions. It is often claimed that the restrictive fifth-freedom policy has been a major factor responsible for the underdeveloped intraregional routes, particularly transcontinental routes, both east–west and north–south. Each nation's carrier is generally allowed to serve only the thin third- and fourth-freedom markets, with no access to behind or beyond traffic. Recognizing this drawback of the regulatory policy, the African Civil Aviation Conference (AFCAC) has been promoting for some time a relaxation of fifth-freedom traffic rights for airlines based in Africa—and for non-African airlines if such rights in Africa are exchanged for reciprocal rights, including compensation. Sixth-freedom traffic is not of much value to the carriers based in Africa because of the location of Africa and the nature of traffic flows. However, such traffic has a significant value for carriers based in other regions, such as the Middle East and Europe.

Regulations regarding nonscheduled operations are of concern only to a limited number of nations, but such services do pose conflicting requirements on the governments. On the one hand, governments are interested in promoting tourism, which warrants more liberal policies. On the other hand, the governments feel the need to protect their scheduled airlines. Such conflicts have precluded the development of uniform rules and regulations for nonscheduled services.

Markets

Although the airlines in Africa have grown at a rate higher than the world average, their share of the total world traffic is still only 2.7 percent of the total ton-kilometers performed in 1985. This share represents an improvement of two-tenths of one percentage point over 1976.[10]

Through-plane scheduled service is available in less than one-fourth of all possible city-pair combinations among the fifty two nations and two dependent territories. Intraregional routes in the western, eastern, and northern subregions are the most developed. The least developed routes are those between the western and eastern subregions and those between the northern and central subregions. For example, as of November 1, 1986, there were only five direct flights per week from Addis Ababa in east Africa to Abidjan in west Africa. Each flight made two or three intermediate stops. On another transcontinental route, from Addis Ababa to Dakar, there was only one direct flight per week, and it made two intermediate stops. As for through-plane services between Africa and other parts of the world, the most developed routes are between northern Africa, Europe, and the Middle East. Central Africa has almost no through-plane service to any other region outside of Africa, except limited service to Europe. Eastern Africa is connected fairly well with the Asia-Pacific region and western Africa with North America. Service to Latin America and the Caribbean is poor from all subregions of Africa.

The demand for air travel, particularly personal travel, has been influenced by migration patterns and religious orientation. For example, the ICAO report on Africa cites three different migration patterns that have influenced the flow of airline traffic. First, the long-established immigrant communities from Western Europe, the Middle East, and Asia generate demand for air travel back to the immigrants' countries of origin. Second, the movement of migrant labor from north Africa (particularly Algeria, Morocco, and Tunisia) to Western Europe (particularly France) has stimulated the demand for air services. Third, migration to the oil-producing countries (both within Africa and in the Middle East) has also influenced air travel demand.[11] In addition to these factors, there remains a certain residual community of interest with Europe (Belgium, France, Germany, Great Britain, Italy, Portugal, and Spain) as a remnant of colonial rule. Finally, the significantly strong association with the Middle East is a result of religious ties. About one-third of the population—mostly in northern Africa and in Ethiopia, Nigeria, and Tanzania—recognizes the Islamic religion, and many followers participate in annual pilgrimages to the Middle East.

More than half of the total international travel to Africa is to destinations in northern Africa. Within this subregion, about half of the countries are popular tourist destinations. The three largest countries included in this group are Egypt, Morocco, and Tunisia. The other half of the countries in the subregion are predominantly destinations for business travelers. Examples include Algeria, Libyan Arab Jamahiriya, and Sudan. In return, the northern subregion is an important generator of the Hadj traffic to Saudi Arabia. After the northern subregion, the western and eastern subregions are about equal in importance in terms of demand for air travel from regions outside Africa. Eastern Africa has more tourist destinations (such as Kenya), whereas the western subregion has a higher percentage of business travel. The central subregion has the lowest number of foreign visitors.

The development of markets by most airlines in the region has been limited to providing domestic services and competitive service to foreign capitals, usually those associated with a previous colonial presence. Less than 15 percent of the total international scheduled passengers traveling to, from, and within Africa are traveling on intraregional routes. More than 85 percent are traveling to and from other regions of the world. About two-thirds of the intraregional travelers move within their subregions, and about one-third travel among the five subregions. Of the total international passengers traveling between Africa and other regions of the world, about 75 percent are traveling to and from Europe, about 20 percent to and from the Middle East, and only about 5 percent to and from all other areas. Further disaggregation of the interregional traffic flows shows that the northern subregion accounts for more than five times the traffic to and from the western subregion and substantially more than the traffic to and from the other three subregions.

One important flow of migrant labor has been from the North African countries to Europe, especially France.[12] Airline passenger traffic over the past ten years has grown at about 7.5 percent per year between North Africa and Europe and at more than 10 percent per year on routes serving the Middle East. Egypt has supplied its work force in large numbers to other Arab countries, which accounts for the high traffic flows to and from Egypt and for the growth of Egyptair.

Table 5–4 presents passenger traffic statistics for the ten busiest African airports during 1985. Clearly, most of the aviation activity takes place at airports located in the northern subregion. Cairo is the leading airport in terms of international passenger traffic. During 1985, twenty-nine foreign cities were served from Cairo with more than ten passengers per day. Of these twenty-nine markets from Cairo, thirteen are in Europe, seven are in the Middle East, five are in the Asia-Pacific region, three are in Africa, and one is in North America. Even from Cairo, there were only three city pairs in Africa with more than ten passengers per day as on-board traffic load. Similar observations can be made for traffic flows from the other major airports shown in table 5–4.

Table 5–4
Passenger Traffic at the Top Ten Airports in Africa, 1985

City	Passengers (000) (embarked plus disembarked)	
	International	*Total*
Cairo	5,124	6,235
Algiers[a]	2,247	3,807
Tunis	1,875	2,030
Johannesburg	1,559	4,462
Tripoli[a]	1,309	2,299
Lagos[a]	1,249	3,282
Casablanca	995[b]	NA
Nairobi	905	1,133
Abidjan	700[b]	NA
Dakar	596[b]	NA

Sources: International Civil Aviation Organization (ICAO), *Civil Aviation Statistics of the World* (Montreal: ICAO, August 1986); and *International Air Passenger and Freight Transport: Africa* (Montreal: ICAO, March 1985).

[a]1984 data.
[b]1982 data.

In addition to the demand for scheduled air travel, there are significant charter markets in northern Africa (Egypt, Morocco, and Tunisia) and south of the Sahara (Central African Republic, Gambia, Kenya, Reunion, Senegal, Togo, and Burkina Faso).[13] Charter traffic from Africa to other regions is primarily to Jidda, Saudi Arabia, for the annual Hadj pilgrimage. Charter traffic accounts for about 10 percent of the total international scheduled traffic, and about four-fifths of this traffic is transported by the scheduled airlines.

Fares

Besides using the mechanisms of the IATA, airlines in Africa also coordinate their fare activities through the African Airline Association (AFRAA). Some members of AFRAA are also members of the Arab Air Carriers Organization (AACO), and these two organizations hold joint meetings to discuss Middle East–Africa fares before they are discussed at the larger IATA meetings. In the past, a number of African airlines have experienced difficulties in reaching agreements on interregional fares. For example, an airline handicapped by operating restrictions might have proposed lower fares to offset the lower quality of its service. In the late 1970s, to facilitate the fare coordination process without compromising the needs and requirements of the regional airlines, AFRAA suggested, with the support of the African Civil Aviation Conference (AFCAC), the establishment of the African Air Tariff Conference (AFRATC) to strengthen the coordination process even further. The purpose of this organization is to agree on tariffs for routes within Africa and to develop proposals for African airlines—to be discussed at the IATA meetings—for routes to and from Africa.

At the intergovernmental level, fares are monitored by AFCAC, which has developed two model bilateral air transport agreements as guidelines for the African nations in their bilateral negotiations. In the model dealing with intraregional bilateral agreements, the tariff clause calls for fares to be agreed through the AFRATC process. In the model dealing with interregional bilateral agreements, the tariff clause calls for fares to be agreed through the IATA process. In both cases, the need for government approval of the agreed fares is implied.

Normal economy fares between Africa and other parts of the world traditionally have been above the world average for all distance groups. The percentage markup has varied from region to region and, in some cases, by direction. As in other regions of the world, a variety of discount fares are available—some officially and some through clandestine channels. In addition, discount fares are available to certain categories of travelers, such as "artists, diplomats, members of the clergy, military personnel, persons with certain handicaps, property owners, ships' crew, sportsmen, students, teachers, and youths."[14] It should be obvious that with very little creativity, almost anyone should be able to fit in a category that qualifies for some discount. In a survey carried out by the ICAO in 1982, the data showed, in fact, that only between 20 and 50 percent of the passengers traveled on normal economy fares between the major cities in Europe and Africa. Therefore, on the average, more than half of the passengers are able to obtain some sort of discount fare. For example, during the period from August 1982 to July 1983, the following percentages of passengers utilized the intermediate class and normal economy class between France and various subregions of Africa: northern Africa, 38 percent; western Africa, 26 percent; central Africa, 41 percent; and eastern Africa, 25 percent.[15]

Local fares between countries within Africa appear to be below the world average for comparable distances (see table 5–5). In all cases, local fares in Africa ranged from 14 to 28 percent below the world average. The ICAO sample included 543 city pairs within the area composed of the continent of Africa and offshore islands but excluded Algeria, the Canary Islands, Egypt, Madeira, Malta, Morocco, Sudan, and Tunisia. Fares on individual routes vary from subregion to subregion. This is in great contrast to Europe, where local normal economy fares are significantly higher than the world average, even though European markets generally have much higher traffic densities.

Financial Performance

The financial performance of carriers based in Africa has been dismal relative to the world average. The African airline industry as a whole has trouble achieving breakeven status on an operating basis, let alone on a net basis. The African airline industry's financial performance on a net basis is even worse, since nonoperating costs tend to be high compared to those in other regions of the world. During the past ten years, while all airlines have been affected by factors such as recessions and changes in the price of oil, the financial performance of airlines in Africa has been influenced adversely by

Table 5–5
Comparison of Average Normal Economy Fares per Kilometer in Africa, September 1985

Route Group	Cents/Kilometer by Distance (km)				
	250	500	1,000	2,000	4,000
Local Africa	20.7	17.8	15.4	13.3	11.4
Int'l total—World	28.7	23.6	19.4	16.0	13.2
Africa as a percentage of world	72	75	79	83	86

Source: International Civil Aviation Organization (ICAO), *Survey of International Air Transport Fares and Rates, September 1985* (Montreal: ICAO, June 1986), 16.

a number of additional factors, such as insufficient foreign exchange, weak domestic economies, burdensome levels of external debt, and competition from larger and better-positioned foreign airlines. Furthermore, many smaller airlines based in Africa compete against the larger foreign airlines that have established worldwide reputations and extensive route networks. The smaller airlines from Africa tend to serve only their local markets and therefore are vulnerable to economic changes in the local markets. The poor performance of many carriers has led to calls for such airlines to be privatized. Such movements are under way in a number of countries, such as Nigeria, Sierra Leone, Sudan, and Zaire.

Although the African carriers usually derive higher unit revenue compared to the world average, they not only experience higher unit operating costs but also achieve lower load factors. In 1983, for example, the airlines based in the AFCAC region reported unit revenues and unit operating costs 18 percent above the world average, measured in U.S. cents per ton-kilometer. However, these airlines achieved a load factor 6 percentage points below the world average.[16] Lower load factors are the result of lower traffic density of the African routes. It is also important to note that Africa's low load factors are in smaller airplanes. The overcapacity in these sparse markets does not exist because the carriers are operating excessively large airplanes or at high frequency.

Table 5–6 shows a comparison of various cost elements for African car-

Table 5–6
Unit Operating Costs of African Airlines Compared with the World Average, 1983
(U.S. cents per ton-kilometer available)

Item	African Airlines[a]	World Average
Overall operating costs	50.6	42.8
Flight crew costs	3.0	3.2
Flight equipment insurance	0.5	0.2
Rental of flight equipment	0.5	0.6
Depreciation and amortization	4.8	3.0
Interest	1.2	1.6
Maintenance and overhaul	4.9	4.1
Aircraft fuel and oil	15.4	10.1
User charges and station expenses	5.8	6.5
Passenger services	3.8	3.8
Ticketing, sales, and promotion	6.2	6.8
General, administrative, and other	4.5	2.9

Source: Data provided by the International Civil Aviation Organization.
[a]Data are for scheduled airlines in the AFCAC region.

riers and all airlines. African airlines clearly have a disadvantage in the following cost categories: flight equipment, insurance, depreciation, maintenance and overhaul; fuel and oil; and general, administrative, and other. The cost disadvantage in the last category is the result of lower staff productivity. Also, although salaries are lower for local staff, they can, in fact, be higher for the expatriate staff. However, administrative costs must be examined in the context of national social and economic goals, especially in relation to employment policies. There are, of course, wide variations in the operations of African carriers. Airlines based in northern Africa, for instance, achieve higher utilization than those based in other subregions.

The acquisition of ill-suited airplanes has contributed to the operational, technical, and economic problems of Africa-based airlines. At times, prior equipment decisions have been dictated by political considerations. At other times, they have been dictated by investments and prefinancing terms and conditions. In any event, the widespread use of inefficient aircraft is a continual drain on the carriers' limited financial resources, and it locks in a permanent cost disadvantage relative to other international carriers.

Barriers to Progress

As already noted, although this region has achieved growth rates in excess of world averages, its total share of the world commercial air transportation market is fairly small. Moreover, the financial performance of the airlines based in this region has been well below the performance of the airlines based in other regions of the world. In almost all cases, the deficits of the state-owned airlines have been offset by government subsidy, on the premise that these airlines are instruments of national policy and a source of national pride and prestige. However, if this region expects to increase its share of the world travel market, improve the financial viability of its airlines, and reduce their dependence on state subsidy, it is necessary to remove a number of barriers. These barriers to progress in African air transportation include (1) a paucity of qualified personnel, (2) limited infrastructure facilities, (3) obsolescent fleets, (4) inadequate financial resources, and (5) social and political constraints.

High-quality management and operational skills have always been essential for successful airline operations. However, they are particularly crucial in this area because of the severe operating constraints. Unfortunately, many African airlines do not have the resources—including qualified staffs—to deal with this highly dynamic and complex industry. Furthermore, besides a lack of formal training and qualifications, there is also a severe shortage of personnel with extensive experience.

In the competitive international aviation environment, there is a critical need to perform comprehensive route profitability analysis, aircraft evaluation, aircraft economic studies, and facilities planning (airports, hangars, and maintenance). Such studies require extensive knowledge of analytical techniques plus voluminous quantities of market research and cost data. In addition, profitable operations require a staff with know-how in automation to manage yield in a cost-effective manner.

There are a number of reasons for the dearth of qualified airline personnel in the region. Part of the problem may be the fact that airlines cannot have their own wage structures and personnel policies. African airline employees are considered civil servants and are compensated as such. Moreover, in the area of technical operations, even when qualified staff are available in one area, there are problems in transferring them between carriers because of national regulations that are not standardized. In other words, there is no reciprocal recognition of regulatory procedures and licensing with respect to technical staff.

The second obstacle to progress is inadequacies in the infrastructure. Limitations exist in the airports and tourism components of the aviation industry. For example, many airports have short runways, inadequate navigational aides, deficient communication equipment, primitive terminal facilities, and substandard fueling facilities. The lack of adequate operational equipment and facilities causes delays and financial losses to airlines and inconvenience to passengers and shippers. A major shortcoming among many African carriers is the inability to fully facilitate the efficient processing of passengers. Successful passenger service requires the availability of adequate accommodations, access, and efficient airport operations. In addition, effective development of the tourism industry requires effective facilitation procedures and practices. Basic improvements are needed in the liberalization of entry visa requirements and the awareness among airport and customs authorities of the need to facilitate airline activity.

An increasingly obsolete fleet is the third obstacle to progress in this region. A large percentage of the fleet is economically inefficient and environmentally unacceptable. The ability to compete effectively in some of the long-haul markets requires modern airplanes. Furthermore, modern airplanes will soon be required to comply with worldwide noise regulations. Unfortunately, not only are such airplanes expensive, but they tend to have large capacities for the size of the markets. Consequently, airlines in this region need to find cost-effective ways to acquire and utilize modern airplanes. Replacing aged airplanes will not solve all the problems of the airlines, however. They also must invest large amounts in infrastructure, such as ground and maintenance equipment and facilities.

The fourth barrier to progress is the very limited financial resources available to the airline industry to replace the first-generation jet airplanes and to expand and modernize airport facilities. Although every airline faces the problem of finding capital to replace existing airplanes, airlines in developing countries face the added problem of making the payment in "hard currency," which inevitably has a negative impact on the balance of payments and, in some cases, make them unable to pay their debts. Moreover, a number of airlines from the developing countries do not consider the terms and conditions of the loans from the World Bank to be reasonable, and they are calling for the establishment of a regional financing agency that would provide much longer term loans at considerably lower interest rates.

Leasing has allowed some undercapitalized airlines to acquire airplanes, but the equipment acquired has not always been ideally suited to the routes served. Moreover, some African airlines prefer to wet-lease airplanes, because the airplanes come with qualified crews. Even for leasing airplanes, some airlines in the region are interested in different terms and conditions that better reflect the operating environment in this area. This concern has led the African Civil Aviation Conference (AFCAC) to promote the establishment of a financing agency for African airlines under the structure of the African Development Bank to provide long-term loans at lower interest rates for airlines to replace their fleets. However, the lack of capital may be somewhat of a blessing in disguise. It may force some airlines to lower their sights and buy more appropriate airplanes instead of the latest and the largest.

Social and political constraints represent the fifth obstacle to progress in the airline industry in this region. The benefits of state ownership are not free. Airlines are expected to conform to government policies, which often conflict with an airline's main objectives. For example, political influences, nepotism, and favoritism in manpower selection often place individuals in senior positions without the necessary skills and experience to perform their functions. In addition, political considerations very often interfere with fleet acquisition decisions. Finally, different kinds of government systems have become obstacles to the development of effective cooperative arrangements, which in this region are essential ingredients for survival—particularly in the smaller nations, in which diseconomies of scale are causing problems. Clearly, political control and interference have been detrimental, and selective loosening of government controls could probably result in improved efficiency and financial performance among the national carriers.

Future Prospects

Although the airline industry in Africa will still be influenced by many external factors—such as the growth in the regional economy, international trade, tourism, and balance of payments—radical changes can be brought about only through the development of multinational, or at least transnational, airlines with strong hubs at strategic locations in each of the subregions. Such a solution cannot be implemented, however, without the will and actions of governments. Unfortunately, strong nationalistic attitudes, political considerations, ideological and cultural differences, and the fear that benefits will not be shared fairly and equitably will effectively counter efforts to increase cooperation for the foreseeable future. The airlines themselves can only go so far to improve their economic viability and further develop the air transportation system. For example, the only opportunities for cooperative efforts among the airlines are in group insurance, economic research, training, computer facilities, equipment inventory, and maintenance. Cooperation and coordination in such areas will be helpful, but they will not solve the airlines' structural problems, such as insufficient resources and low traffic densities.

As owners and regulators, governments bear the burden of change, but they face a difficult choice. Weak domestic economies, reduced export revenues, and diminishing foreign aid will hinder government support of the airline industry at traditional levels. Furthermore, African governments also recognize (1) that worldwide regulatory constraints are being relaxed to varying degrees and at varying paces, (2) that they must harmonize their policies with those in other parts of the world to continue to be a part of the total system, (3) that government-owned flag carriers are extremely expensive, and (4) that the multilateral regulatory process has weakened, and regionalism could be a way to protect the interests of the region and at the same time provide an antidote to strong competition from the outside. On the other hand, making their national airlines economically self-sufficient and positioning them to compete effectively with foreign airlines involves regional cooperation, which could jeopardize the national identities of such airlines and might require that nationalistic attitudes and priorities take a back seat.

The framework for cooperative effort already exists. The 1980 conference of the Organization of African Unity (OAU), held in Lagos, adopted a plan of action for the economic development of Africa based on the principles of collective self-reliance—to be implemented through progressive harmonization of regional and subregional policies and promotion of joint projects. Regional groupings already exist in the western, central, and southern subregions to promote regional integration on economic fronts. For example, the Southern African Development Coordination Conference (SADCC) was formed (including Angola, Botswana, Lesotho, Malawi, Mozambique, Swaziland, Tanzania, Zambia, and Zimbabwe) to improve joint economic conditions and, presumably, to free the signatories from South Africa's economic control. This regional organization already has established the Southern African Transport and Communications Commission (SATCC) to assist in the establishment of regionally based industries.

If, as is claimed, the SADCC is set on a course to become self-sufficient with respect to transportation and communication infrastructures, then it is not unreasonable to assume that the southern subregion could propose the development of a strong multinational airline, with strategically located hub-and-spoke systems. Such a system would circumvent the small traffic base dilemma of the individual partners by pooling their national markets into a subregional common market. Problems in establishing and maintaining common air travel market arrangements within the subregion are not insurmountable if the political will exists. Furthermore, if the benefits can be distributed fairly and equitably, there is a realistic prospect for significant success. However, for reasons cited earlier—plus the unsuccessful outcome of a previous attempt at a subregional economic and business entity (the East African Community and East African Airways) and the uncertain status of existing multinational airlines in other developing regions—the development of subregional multinational airlines probably is not politically feasible at this time.

Given current trends, it appears that, for the foreseeable future, African air transport will continue to be a small part of total world aviation activity, with the Africa-based airlines struggling against major disadvantages. The fact that the African airlines conduct the bulk of their business in other regions against airlines that are more efficient, coupled with the likelihood of reduced government subsidy and costly compliance with worldwide noise requirements, is forcing African airlines into minimizing costs and maximizing revenues.

Cost improvements will most likely be achieved through improved productivity, pooled resources, restructured fleets, and joint purchases (fuel, airplane insurance). At the operational level, considerable advantages can be derived by sharing airplanes for thin routes or highly seasonal routes. Such decisions, however, call for standard airplanes, standard crew training, and, to some extent, a loss of identity. Leasing may help overcome some of these obstacles, besides providing other benefits, such as avoiding large capital requirements and, in the case of wet leases, avoiding the need for trained staff. In other parts of the world, automation has helped to improve operating efficiency. However, automation in the African airline industry must be examined very carefully. Cost-effectiveness is the key consideration; and inasmuch as labor is relatively cheap and abundant, an optimal balance in Africa may be relatively labor-intensive. Similarly, the implementation of schemes and infrastructure designed for advanced airlines may not be applicable in Africa, since socioeconomic characteristics differ among emerging and advanced countries. For example, can automated ticketing be justified if the volume of traffic is low?

Improvements in revenue are most likely to come from increased airplane utilization, improved load factors, and the development of feeder services and ancillary services (hotels, surface transportation, and time-sharing on computers). In addition to improving utilization by the use of shared airplanes, utilization can also be improved by the use of hub-and-spoke feeder systems. In the absence of regional hub-and-spoke systems designed to accommodate the needs of multinational airline operations, it is likely that individual airlines will develop their own cost-effective hub-and-spoke systems and will coordinate their schedules with other airlines to overcome the obstacle of limited traffic densities. The effectiveness of these hubs will depend heavily on the regulated constraints on developing ideal route structures. In other words, to what extent will government attitudes be relaxed to allow the development of transborder traffic to feed hubs? A more liberal exchange of route rights within Africa would be beneficial to airlines and passengers and could ultimately lead to the development of transcontinental routes. An obvious way for governments to help their airlines boost revenues would be greater cooperation in the area of surplus revenue—that is, allowing African carriers to "bring home" revenues generated within Africa.

Although there are limitations on the cost-minimization and revenue-enhancement strategies that airlines in Africa can implement, experience in other regions has shown the importance of the following considerations. First, it is usually more effective to pool talents as well as resources. Second, it is more beneficial to build on an airline's or nation's structural advantages, such as tourism. And third, it is necessary to examine all aspects of a strategy. For example, a decision to promote tourism will require the development of charter markets, with or without the national airline. Such a strategy may also call for an improvement in the infrastructure and the facilitation process. Cargo transport is another example. It cannot be expanded effectively until there are adequate facilities, such as warehousing, security at the airport, and tracing capability. In addition, it is necessary to eliminate institutional barriers, such as high customs duties.

In summary, the question that is being asked in the African airline industry is not *whether* government and airline policies should change to be consistent with the evolutionary changes in the world's marketplace, but rather the extent to which and the pace at which they should change. This region's airlines will not agree to a fare policy based only on the costs of efficient foreign airlines, but neither can they ignore the fact that they will be operating against those carriers in a competitive environment. In the final analysis, it appears that there will be increased cooperation on technical and operational fronts among the individual airlines but that cooperation in economic areas will be carefully scrutinized and closely controlled by the owner governments, which will continue to protect their national carriers in order to pursue a predetermined national agenda.

Notes

1. Robin Luckham, "Political and Social Problems of Development," in *Africa: South of the Sahara, 1987*, 16th ed. (London: Europa Publications, 1987), 47.

2. Paolo Logli, "Industry in Africa," in *Africa: South of the Sahara, 1987,* 16th ed. (London: Europa Publications, 1987), 68.

3. Luckham, "Political and Social Problems," 42.

4. Europa, *The Europa Year Book 1986* (London: Europa Publications, 1986), 53.

5. Nick Fadugba, "African Carriers," in *1985/1986 Airfinance Annual* (London: Airfinance Journal, 1986), 79–81.

6. Luckham, "Political and Social Problems," 41.

7. International Civil Aviation Organization (ICAO), *Africa: International Air Passenger and Freight Transport* (Montreal: ICAO, March 1985), 24.

8. Gideon H. Kaunda, "Regulation—A Government Perspective," in *Future Challenges in African Air Transport* (Geneva: IATA, June 1985), 37–59.

9. ICAO, *Africa,* 35.

10. International Civil Aviation Organization (ICAO), *Bulletin* (Montreal: ICAO, June 1986), 25.

11. ICAO, *Africa.*

12. David Woolley, "Civil Aviation in Africa: Struggling Against Major Disadvantages," *Interavia,* September 1983, 917–22.

13. ICAO, *Africa,* 24.

14. Ibid., 76.

15. Ibid., 127–28.

16. African Civil Aviation Conference (AFCAC), *A Working Paper,* Presented at the Ninth Plenary Session, Niamey, May 21–June 1, 1985.

6
The Asia-Pacific Region

During the past two decades, there has been a gradual shift in the distribution of scheduled air traffic among the International Civil Aviation Organization's six regions in favor of the Asia-Pacific region. During the ten-year period from 1976 to 1985, the share of scheduled international air traffic of North American and European carriers decreased from 64.1 percent to 57.4 percent of all international traffic. The share of the international scheduled air traffic carried by the airlines registered in the Asia-Pacific region increased from 19.6 percent to 26.7 percent. As figure 6–1 shows, the total scheduled airline traffic accounted for by the Asia-Pacific region is beginning to approach the level achieved by Europe. Between 1975 and 1985, passenger traffic volume grew at a compounded annual growth rate of about 6 percent for Europe, compared to about 11 percent for the Asia-Pacific region. This shift in regional shares is the result of numerous macro- and microeconomic developments, including (1) high-growth export-oriented economies that, until recently, have been more recession-resistant; (2) highly productive, low-cost airlines that have creatively marketed an aggressively priced, high-quality product and have become world-class airlines; (3) greater coordination and cooperation between the airlines and their respective governments; (4) U.S. procompetitive policies initiated during the Carter administration; and (5) a willingness on the part of the Japanese government to pursue more procompetitive policies.

Based on historical trends in airline traffic, the region's premier economic growth, and the emerging growth potential of the Chinese and Indian air transport markets, the Asia-Pacific region has often been characterized as the "future dynamo" of the international civil aviation industry. However, although some parts of this region—such as South Korea, Taiwan, and China—represent a considerable economic opportunity for continued growth in trade and investment (and therefore in air transportation activity), duplication of past growth trends in export trade in some of the same countries also represents a potential threat to other industrially developed regions, such as North America and Europe. It is therefore quite possible that before this region be-

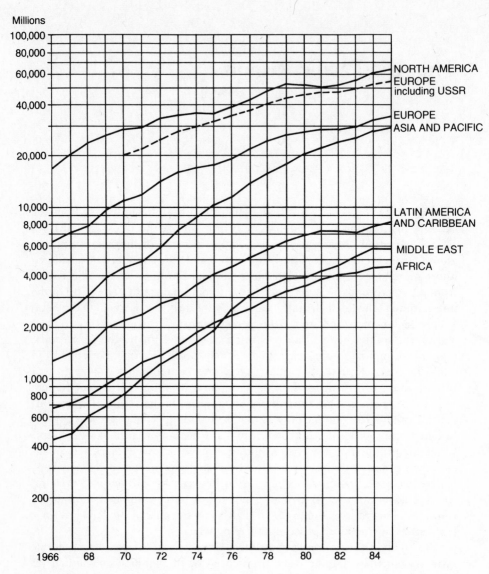

Source: International Civil Aviation Organization (ICAO), *Bulletin* (Montreal: ICAO, June 1986), 26.

Figure 6–1. Long-Term Regional Air Traffic Trends (growth in ton-kilometers)

comes the largest component of the world's economy (and, in turn, the world's passenger market), it may provoke restrictionist economic and/or administrative policies in the North American and European nations. Recent experience supports the hypothesis that protectionist policies are beginning to have some impact on economies in the region. Some of this region's economies are beginning to see their first major setbacks, and others have achieved actual growth well below forecast levels.

This chapter provides a synthesis and assessment of both the past and the likely future developments in the Asia-Pacific region. Because so much of this region's air transportation potential is tied to the area's emerging world economies, the spotlight in this chapter is on the past and future economic conditions in this region and on some critical factors inherent in the leading countries in the region that could affect the future demand for air transportation services. Since this region represents a huge area, most of the discussion is limited to a subset of the region commonly known as the Asian Pacific Rim, which comprises ten major countries. These ten countries, which account for the vast majority of the region's air travel, are further divided into four groups in terms of income levels: (1) Japan; (2) four newly industrializing countries (NICs) in east Asia—Hong Kong, Singapore, South Korea, and Taiwan; (3) four members of the Association of Southeast Asian Nations (ASEAN)—Indonesia, Malaysia, the Philippines, and Thailand; and (4) the People's Republic of China.[1]

Economic Characteristics of the Region

The Asia-Pacific region is an extremely diverse and far-flung region comprising a broad spectrum of independent nations with different cultural, political, and economic traits. According to the ICAO definition, the Asia-Pacific region, comprising thirty-four nations (as well as the dependent territories of several extraregional nations), extends west to include the Indian subcontinent, east to include Korea and Japan, north to include China, and south to include Australia, New Zealand, and the South Pacific (see figure 6–2). The ICAO further divides the region into four subregions (western, central, northeastern, and southeastern). Table 6–1 lists the nations and territories in each of these four subregions. Two of the four subregions contain 86 percent of the area's total population (northeastern, 47 percent, and western, 39 percent). In 1980, eleven of the twenty-five most populous cities in the world were in the Asia-Pacific region. By the end of this century, fourteen cities in the region are expected to be in the top twenty-five.[2]

In 1983, the Asia-Pacific region as a whole accounted for 56 percent of the world's population, 22 percent of the world's gross national product, and 19 percent of total world trade by value. Although the average GNP per

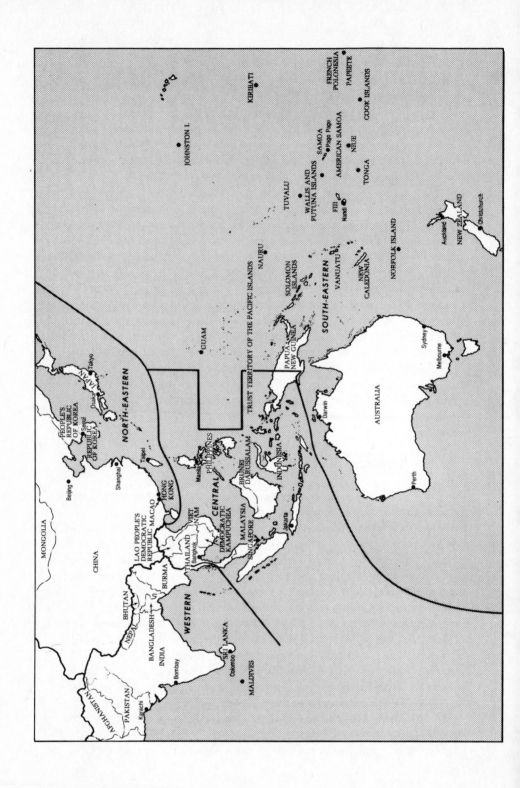

Table 6–1
Nations and Territories of the ICAO Asia-Pacific Region

Western Subregion
Nations
Afghanistan
Bangladesh
Bhutan[a]
Burma
India
Maldives
Nepal
Pakistan
Sri Lanka

Central Subregion
Nations
Brunei Darussalam
Democratic Kampuchea
Indonesia
Lao People's Democratic Republic
Malaysia
Philippines
Singapore
Thailand
Viet Nam

Northeastern Subregion
Nations
China
Democratic People's Republic of Korea
Japan
Mongolia[a]
Republic of Korea

Territories
Hong Kong
Macao

Southeastern Subregion
Nations
Australia
Fiji
Kiribati
Nauru
New Zealand
Papua New Guinea
Samoa[a]
Solomon Islands
Tonga
Tuvalu[a]
Vanuatu

Territories
American Samoa
Cook Islands
French Polynesia
Guam
New Caledonia
Niue
Norfolk Island
Trust Territory of the Pacific Islands
Wallis and Futuna Islands

Source: International Civil Aviation Organization (ICAO), *International Air Passenger and Freight Transport* (Montreal: ICAO, September 1986), 119.
[a]Noncontracting state of the ICAO.

capita ($925) is comparable to that in Africa ($754) and considerably less than that in North America ($13,873), it is very high for some countries—such as Australia ($10,780), Japan ($10,100), and Singapore ($6,620)—and very low for other countries—such as Bangladesh, Bhutan, and the Lao People's Republic (between $100 and $150). Clearly, the region's economic wealth is highly concentrated. Just four nations (Australia, China, India, and

Japan) account for 82 percent of the region's GNP. Not only is Japan the second largest economic power in the world, but it accounts for more than half of the region's total GNP.[3]

During the past two decades, the four groups of Asia-Pacific nations discussed in this chapter have made substantial strides toward becoming major world centers of economic activity. Although individual countries within each group have reported different growth rates, even the countries recording low growth have outpaced, by a wide margin, the growth experienced by the United States and leading countries in Western Europe. Of course, this region's growth rate comparisons are somewhat misleading because they are calculated against a much smaller baseline, but if economic growth continues at the same rate during the next two decades, this subset of the region could account for a share of the world production comparable to that of the United States. The end result would be enormous intraregional trade flows as well as increased trade flows between these Asia-Pacific countries and both North America and Europe.

Air transportation plays an important role in the Asia-Pacific region for four reasons: geography, economic activity, population, and tourism. In terms of geography, many countries in the region are island or archipelago nations. Furthermore, there are vast distances between countries within the region, which extends from Kabul to Papeete (a distance of 16,000 km) and from Tokyo to Sydney (a distance of 7,800 km). About 60 percent of the city pairs receiving through-plane service are at least 2,000 km apart.[4] Second, the growth in external trade has led to a need for more air transportation services. Third, even though the region's per capita volume of air traffic is only about half the world average, the size and growth of population point to an increasing demand for air transportation services. Fourth, tourism has become a vital economic enterprise for a number of countries in this region, and air transportation is a more integral part of tourism in this region than in other regions in the world. The island and archipelago nations can be reached only by air. The contiguous nations that are attractive tourist centers are far removed from wealthy populations.

Japan

The most important country in the Asian Pacific Rim—in terms of strength of the economy as well as strength of airline traffic—is, of course, Japan. Although small in land size and poor in natural resources, Japan now ranks second behind the United States in gross national product. And if the historical growth rates continue, Japan's economy will surpass that of the United States by the end of this century. The export component has been the primary force in the growth of the Japanese economy. Japan now enjoys a massive trade surplus (about $50 billion in 1985 with the United States alone), an enormously strong yen, and a disposable income per capita that is approaching the levels enjoyed in the United States and Western Europe.

The important question now is whether the Japanese economy will continue to grow at the same rate as it has in the decades past. Recent developments indicate that this will not be the case. As already mentioned, many Western industrialized countries have unfavorable trade imbalances with Japan. To reduce such imbalances, and to protect domestic industries, North American and European governments may feel compelled to implement restrictionist trade policies. These countries are already pressuring Japan to institute voluntary economic policies that place greater emphasis on domestic demand and less on export demand and that allow greater accessibility to Japan's domestic markets for imports from other countries. Even with such voluntary actions, there is an increasing probability that foreign protectionist policies will be implemented that will severely affect Japanese trade and growth. Moreover, countries within the Asia-Pacific region are also putting pressure on Japan for access to its domestic markets, albeit for different economic reasons. Now that Japan is an economic dynamo, other countries, both within and outside the region, want to increase their trade with Japan to bolster their own economies. However, most of the other countries in the region have very little demand for Japan's high-value-added manufactured products. Therefore, such trade is likely to be very one-sided, to Japan's detriment.

A 1986 U.S. Congressional Research Service report mentions a number of other factors that support the hypothesis that the Japanese economy will experience slower growth. First, following World War II, the Japanese government not only provided economic and financial incentives to targeted industries for rapid development but also protected many of these industries from international competition. Meanwhile, the government promoted plenty of competition among domestic firms to ensure that the products that were exported were of high quality and low cost. Nowadays, the government is less effective in exerting the type of control over domestic markets that was possible previously. Second, because it is so heavily dependent on international trade, Japan's economy is becoming less and less independent of economic policies and business conditions in other major countries. As a result, the Japanese economy is becoming more integrated into the world economy and is no longer resistant to recessions in other regions of the world. Third, it is quite clear that as production costs rise in Japan, substantial amounts of labor-intensive production will move to the Asian NICs (South Korea and Taiwan, in particular), where labor costs are about 25 percent of the level in Japan. Fourth, the strength of the yen is making Japanese products more expensive in foreign markets. Together, these four factors are expected to reduce Japan's future economic growth relative to past experience and to result in some restructuring of Japan's economy.

Of course, a restructuring of Japan's economy could also present new opportunities for growth. For example, the gradual shift in production of maturing technologies to lower-cost manufacturing facilities in the NICs is causing Japan to move toward even higher technology industries, such as computers, aerospace, and biotechnology. Second, as exports to North America and Europe begin to stabilize, Japan has begun to foster the economic potential of other countries in this region (particularly China) and, to a limited extent, in Latin America and Africa as future markets for its products. In time, the Asian market could become comparable to the U.S. and European markets for Japanese products. Third, if Japan continues to pursue its policy of voluntary restraints to circumvent protectionist trade barriers, the Japanese industries could accelerate the expansion of their overseas production to maintain their market shares—that is, establishing more North America–based manufacturing facilities for Japanese-brand products.

Although the Japanese economy will continue to be influenced by the aforementioned positive and negative forces, the overriding criteria will be the continuing trade tensions between the United States and Japan. And the solutions to this conflict will affect not only the economies of both countries and the trade between them but also the opportunities for trade between other countries in the region and Japan and between the United States and Japan.

Regarding air transportation services to and from Japan, that country produces more revenue ton-kilometers per capita and per dollar gross domestic product than any other country in the region. Figure 6–3 shows the traffic pattern to and from Japan during 1984. It appears that the demand for air transportation services is likely to continue to grow on the basis of emerging opportunities as the economy is restructured to adapt to the changing environment. For example, in the past, government policies were directed at strengthening the industrial sector by promoting savings and investment at the expense of personal consumption. A change in economic policy that places a lower emphasis on saving and a higher emphasis on spending is likely to increase the demand for air transportation services. As one observer states: "The country is now mature. Its citizens want what goes with that maturity."[5] Moreover, the strength of the yen relative to other currencies should make foreign travel more attractive for the Japanese. It is also possible, however, that the yen's enormous strength is causing Japanese exporting companies to reduce wages and employment to keep their products competitive in the international marketplace.

Nevertheless, the extent to which Japan can accept more air transportation services (and, in turn, higher growth in traffic) is limited by the ability of the current infrastructure, particularly the capacity of international airports. At present, there are as many countries waiting to get access to airport services at the Narita International airport as there are countries whose air-

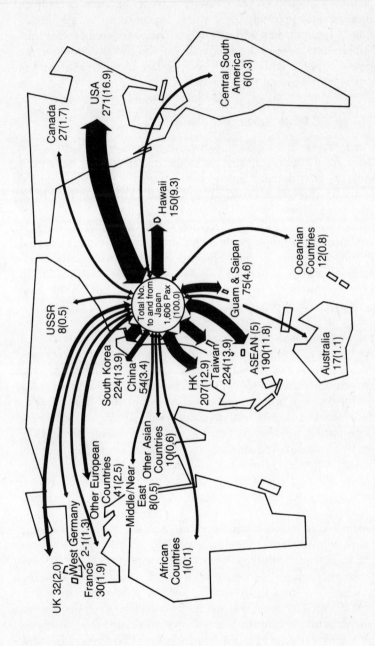

Source: Japan Transport Consultants Association (JTCA), *Information Booklet (1985)*:
Outline of Civil Aviation in Japan (Tokyo: JTCA, 1986), 10.
Note: Unit is ten thousand pax. A figure in parentheses indicates share (%) occupied by
each country (area) of total passenger traffic to and from Japan.

Figure 6–3. Passenger Traffic to and from Japan, 1984 (unit: ten thousand pax)

lines currently provide service at Narita International.[6] Expansion at Narita has been blocked for a number of years, however, partly because several parcels of land continue to be privately held. A new airport to be built in the sea near Osaka (Kansai International Airport) will not be completed until at least 1993, even if all obstacles were to be removed. The forecast slowdown in the Japanese economy, coupled with the lack of adequate airport capacity, will limit the growth in traffic to and from Japan.

Hong Kong, Singapore, South Korea, and Taiwan

As in Japan, the governments of Hong Kong, Singapore, South Korea, and Taiwan also have been supporting private-sector initiatives and have been creating a conducive environment for targeted industries to fulfill national trade and industrialization goals. North America and Europe continue to be vital trading partners of these NICs. They are markets for the NICs' manufactured products—such as clothing, electronics, and machinery—whereas the NICs rely on them for technology, financing, investment, and educational training for technocrats and managers. The high level of growth in the economies of Hong Kong and Singapore has almost raised their classification to developed economies, in that their incomes per capita (about $6,000 and $7,000, respectively) now approach the levels in a number of countries in Western Europe.

Although these four Asian NICs are poor in resources (as Japan is), as a group they have been quite successful in stimulating the growth in their economies by developing their export markets (for example, by increasing the value added to manufactured goods). Taiwan, for example, has been quite successful in shifting a very high percentage of its population from rural to urban areas to concentrate on industrial production; Korea has been very successful in introducing modern technology into its economy; and Hong Kong, having transformed its transit trade to processing trade, has recently been concentrating on the development of information and service industries. The resulting growth in the economies of these countries has raised the GNP per capita significantly (an excellent predictor of the demand for air transportation services).

As a group, these four NICs have accumulated substantial trade surpluses, particularly with the United States, which has been the group's number one market. Total trade with the United States varies from about 20 percent for Singapore to about 40 percent for Taiwan. Consequently, as in the case of Japan, these four Asian NICs could become vulnerable to foreign trade restrictions directed at exports if the trade imbalances became unsustainable; this is particularly true for South Korea and Taiwan, which send about a third of their total exports to the United States. The recent downturn in Taiwan's economy as a result of the reduction in exports to the United

States is just one example of the region's dependence on the vitality of the U.S. market. However, unlike Japan, which was able to implement protectionist import policies without encountering any significant retaliatory measures by foreign governments, these four Asian NICs (particularly South Korea and Taiwan) are being watched carefully by the old industrialized countries so that these "new Japans" do not follow the Japanese growth formula. Moreover, Western countries are now more careful about technology transfer than they were when Japan was expanding its industrial base. On the other hand, these Asian NICs could benefit in the short run from trade restrictions imposed on Japan.

Not only have the major developed economies considered implementing protectionist policies, but the economic growth rates of some of the countries in the region are already showing signs of slowing, even though the U.S. and the Japanese economies are still reporting positive growth. And the area's slowdown may be compounded if Japan or the United States enters another recession. The economic growth of the Philippines has been on a slide since 1980. In 1985, for the first time since independence, Singapore experienced a negative growth in its economy. Recently, there has been a downturn in Taiwan's economy as a result of the reduction in exports to the United States. Apparently, there is a limit to the extent to which various nations in the Asia-Pacific region can replicate Japan's growth formula.

In addition, just as some of these countries are providing low-cost manufacturing competition to Japan, some Asian NICs could also be forced to move higher on the industrialization ladder to combat fierce competition from the ASEAN nations in the production of labor-intensive products. For example, labor costs in Singapore have increased at a rate higher than the increase in productivity (over 10 percent per year compared to less than 5 percent per year between 1978 and 1984), a situation that could reduce Singapore's competitiveness in exported manufactured goods relative to other countries, such as South Korea and Taiwan. Moreover, until now, the value of the currencies of these Asian NICs has been pegged to the value of the U.S. dollar. If a decision is made to untie the value of these currencies from the U.S. dollar—as a means to reduce the U.S. trade deficit—these countries could face problems similar to those faced by Japan. And reductions in export-related revenue not only would have an impact on the general economic future of these countries but would have a tremendous impact on the ability of these countries to earn foreign exchange and attract foreign investments.

The future of Hong Kong after 1997 continues to be a controversial issue. In the 1984 agreement between China and Great Britain, China agreed, at least in theory, to allow Hong Kong to maintain its capitalist economy, representative government, and existing "life style" for a number of years. However, since it is difficult to know precisely what this means, there is a threat of interference from China—interference that could affect the business climate and, eventually, the prosperity of Hong Kong. Given this uncertainty, and despite the fact that the Hong Kong stock market has been showing bullish trends in 1987, and despite the fact that the private sector is willing to commit HK $25 billion to develop a new airport, *Business Week* reports that "most new investments are designed for paybacks in less than ten years."[7]

Although the air travel demand to and from these countries will be negatively affected by the slowdown in the growth of their economies, it will continue to be positively affected by the marketing flair and aggressiveness of their airlines, the availability of expanded airport facilities, and the exploitation of advancing airplane technology (discussed later in this chapter). Singapore Airlines is a good example. The service on Singapore Airlines has been and continues to be cited as one of the best in the world. Now Singapore's airport (Changi) is also cited as one of the most modern airports in the world. And whereas Narita is virtually closed for additional service, Changi is being marketed as a potential hub for other airlines. In addition, Singapore is being marketed as a shopping mecca and a convention center, unlike Japan, where travel costs have become prohibitive.

Indonesia, Malaysia, the Philippines, and Thailand

Unlike the four East Asian NICs, which have limited natural resources, the four ASEAN countries are relatively rich in natural resources, especially petroleum and rubber, but they are also vulnerable to commodity-price uncertainties (for example, both Indonesia and Malaysia are heavily dependent on oil revenues). These countries do have larger populations, however, and their income per capita is considerably less (for example, well under $1,000 in Indonesia and the Philippines, about $2,000 in Malaysia, and about $3,000 in Thailand). In the past two decades, the economic growth of these four ASEAN nations has been less than the rate experienced by the four East Asian NICs, although the slowest growth rate in the region is still twice the rate achieved by the United States and by a number of countries in Europe.

Nonetheless, the four ASEAN countries face greater challenges in the development of their economies compared to the four East Asian NICs. As a group, the ASEAN nations still must keep substantial resources committed to the agricultural sector, leaving limited resources available to be shifted to the manufacturing sector. The development of the export market for manufactured goods is further constrained by two other factors: protection of inefficient industries, leading to uncompetitiveness in the export marketplace; and the large percentage of the output from the manufacturing sector that is consumed domestically. On the positive side, however, just as the increase in wage rates in Japan has benefited the labor-intensive manufacturing sector in the four East Asian NICs, a similar process could benefit the four ASEAN countries as wages increase in the NICs (as exemplified in the case of Singapore). In fact, the high cost of production in Japan and the relative attraction of Thailand as an offshore production platform are inducing many Japanese manufacturers to invest in Thailand. Finally, this group of countries is also restrained by the International Monetary Fund (IMF) austerity policies, though less so in Thailand.

Future prospects for the ASEAN states could improve substantially if they could coordinate their economic policies more sincerely and more squarely and work toward joint ventures and regional cooperation along the lines of the European Economic Community. Unfortunately, although these remain the superficial goals of the ASEAN nations individual countries in the association are establishing policies in their own self-interest, as typified by Malaysia's "go-it-alone development of the Made-in-Malaysia car, the Proton Saga" and "efforts to woo manufacturing out of Singapore."[8] Moreover, some members of this group continue to suffer from disruptive political upheavals.

The demand for air transportation services to and from these countries is obviously much lower than it is in other countries (such as Japan, Australia, Singapore, and Korea) because of lower economic and trade activity. To offset the lower level of demand for business travel, a number of these countries have been attempting to promote tourism, as exemplified by the efforts of Thai Airways. However, even the development of tourism is hindered in some countries by such factors as the lack of infrastructure and the existence of political unrest.

China

In recent years, there has been a great deal of interest in the potential of the People's Republic of China as a major air travel market. The general hypothesis is that China's enormous population base and vast size, coupled with the current government's policies to promote economic growth, could make this country a major economic power and a significant air travel market in the Asia-Pacific region. Greater interest in Western economic and managerial practices, an increasing appetite for higher-technology goods, and a growing appreciation of the benefits of international trade are recent examples of China's efforts to become a more active participant in world affairs. Supposedly, the key ingredients for setting the economy on a growth path are in place. Since the beginning of this decade, the Chinese economy has been undergoing a major restructuring—based, presumably, on the spectacular growth of other countries in the region since the Korean war. Under the leadership of Deng Xiaoping, China appears to have opened its doors and to have begun the process of catching up with its neighbors, a process exemplified by proposed modernization in four areas (agriculture, defense, industry, and technology) and the seventh five-year plan. The five-year plan, initiated in 1986, contains specific goals for economic growth, the development of foreign trade, and the attraction of foreign investment. This five-year plan is particularly important for the aviation industry, because it shows the importance the government has placed on the role of the air transport industry in the modernization of China. For example, the government acknowledges the importance of tourism for earning foreign currency, which is vital if China is to buy foreign goods and services to support the modernization plan. The five-year plan also provides substantial funds for development of the transportation infrastructure (such as airports).

However, although China has been implementing policies to modernize and has opened its doors to trade, investments, and tourism, the frustrations for foreign companies and the forces behind rigid communist policies and practices have by no means disappeared. Forces favoring central planning and orthodox Marxist policies will continue to exist on and off for a long time and will very likely slow down the free-market forces and, in turn, the pace of China's economic reforms and economic growth. Moreover, it could be a very long time before any significant proportion of the population can be shifted from farming to the industrial sector. At present, about four-fifths of the total population belongs to the farming community.

Unlike Japan and the four East Asian NICs, China is a huge country with substantial natural resources. However, although the size of the Chinese total gross domestic product is quite respectable by world standards, the income per capita is very low (about $300). This income per capita is expected to increase significantly as a result of modernization, growth in the economy, and efforts to limit population growth. However, even significant increases in income per capita are not likely to produce substantial increases in travel by the Chinese people, particularly nonbusiness travel. The anticipated gains in income per capita will more likely be used to fulfill the more fundamental needs of the inhabitants. Nevertheless, a growth in the overall economy will undoubtedly increase the demand for business air travel to and from China. In addition, the government's promotion of tourism will increase nonbusiness travel by foreigners.

The Air Transportation System

Air Transport Trends

In recent years, air transportation services to, from, and within the Asia-Pacific region have undergone some dramatic changes:

1. Greater liberalization of regulatory policies;
2. A review of Australia's two-airline policy;

3. Separation of China's civil aviation regulatory and administrative functions;

4. Persistent demands by domestic operators for greater international route authority;

5. Privatization of government-controlled enterprises;

6. Development of efficient long-range aircraft;

7. Relaxation of first-freedom rights by the Soviet government;

8. An increased role for tourism in air transportation markets;

9. Expanded interisland air links among South Pacific nations;

10. As mentioned in chapter 1, United's purchase of Pan American's Pacific routes, which is expected to raise the level of competition in the Asia-Pacific market.

This section provides an overview of these important developments and their implications.

There is a wide variation within the Asia-Pacific region in regulatory policies and in the development of international air transportation. However, the overall direction is toward greater liberalization. According to a recent ICAO study, approximately half of the bilateral agreements signed by the countries in the Asia-Pacific region include capacity arrangements based on the principles of Bermuda One; the other half use predetermination of capacity control. In both cases, capacity and frequencies are usually shared equally between the two partners. Very few countries advocate the free determination approach. Intraregional services have normally been provided by one carrier from each country (single designation), whereas interregional services have been provided by more than one carrier from each country (multiple designation).[9] An example of the latter is the service between Japan and the United States. Until recently, there were multiple carriers from the United States and one carrier from Japan. Now there are multiple carriers from both countries.

Although the region as a whole has been more willing to accept change than Europe has, the rate of change has varied from country to country. Until recently, Japan and Australia have shown extreme conservatism in their regulatory policies, while Singapore has pursued extremely liberal policies for a number of years with respect to routes, capacity, and tariffs. Singapore has even allowed a foreign carrier (Qantas) to establish a hub operation there. Qantas can now fly from a number of cities in Australia to Singapore, where passengers can then connect on a number of Qantas flights destined for major cities in Europe. These differences in regulatory approaches are a function of general economic philosophies and strategic plans, which try to capitalize on strengths and compensate for weaknesses. For instance, Japan has a very large origin and destination traffic base; consequently, its conservative policies are aimed at protecting this valuable asset by making sure that the Japanese carriers have an opportunity to receive their fair share of the market. Singapore, in contrast, has an insignificant origin and destination traffic base relative to the size of its national airline; consequently, the airline has to promote liberal mercantilistic policies to be able to benefit from other nations' third- and fourth-freedom traffic. Australia, unable to slow down the inroads made by the airlines based in the United States, the United Kingdom, and Singapore, and recognizing the higher economic potential of the Pacific relative to Europe, is taking some steps toward liberalization.

Passenger traffic flow to and from North America constitutes the largest component of interregional traffic. Within this market, the United States and Japan is the most important country pair in terms of passenger movements. In fact, the two top passenger markets in the world involving a city in the Asia-Pacific region and one of the other five ICAO regions are Honolulu–Tokyo and Los Angeles–Tokyo. Given the strength of the passenger market between the United States and Japan, the most complex and controversial bilateral agreement has been and continues to be the one between these two countries. Since 1952, when the original agreement was signed, the agreement has been changed in small increments many times to respond to changes in the environment. However, it has not been possible to incorporate major changes in the agreement because of fundamental disagreement between the two partners with respect to the balance of economic benefits. In general, the Japanese believe that the Americans derive greater economic benefits from the agreement than they do. Conversely, the United States feels that the economic benefits are not imbalanced and that its desire to revise the bilateral agreement is based on the need to make the agreement more flexible so as to provide both partners with greater opportunities. In recent years, there has been a definite shift in policy from protection and restrictions to less government control. There are at least three reasons for this shift in policy: worldwide pressure to liberalize; commercial requirements of Japan Air Lines (for example, domestic routes to feed international services); and the JAL B-747 accident. This shift in policy has resulted in several changes: (1) transfer of Pan American's routes to United; (2) introduction of two additional Japanese carriers on international routes (one combination and one all-cargo); (3) authorization of two additional U.S. combination carriers (American and Delta) on the routes between the two countries; and (4) the decision to privatize Japan Air Lines.

The second change relates to the possibility that the Australian government may abandon its two-airline policy (TAP), which has regulated entry, capacity, and fares in domestic markets. The pressure to revamp TAP has come primarily from four sources: consumer groups, academicians, certain states (for example, South Australia), and a third airline, East West Airlines (EWA). This third airline implemented a lower-fare strategy with the objective of stimulating demand rather than diverting traffic from the existing two domestic airlines. Not satisfied with the route authority provided by the government, EWA has challenged the TAP in the federal courts. Some reforms were introduced in the TAP in 1981, and it has been under further review since then. Even if the TAP is not abandoned, additional reforms are expected, including relaxed operating conditions for the domestic carriers as well as changes for the flag carrier (such as domestic route authority).

A third dramatic change affecting Asia-Pacific air transportation trends is China's move to separate its civil aviation regulatory and administrative functions from airline operations in the Civil Aviation Administration of China (CAAC). This decision could produce a number of separate and relatively strong domestic and international airlines. In the past, the CAAC was responsible not only for the operations and management of the national airline and airports but also for the administration of all civil aviation activities (such as delineation of government aviation policy, negotiation of bilateral agreements, management and operation of the air traffic control system, and investigation of accidents). The divesture of CAAC's functions and responsibilities will improve the efficiency of each component of the aviation system. Specifically, CAAC's airline services have not measured up to the standards provided by other airlines in the world. Greater autonomy, coupled with an improvement in the infrastructure, will result in a strengthening of the national and regional airlines as well as an increase in their share of air travel to, from, and within China.

The fourth change relates to the trend whereby a number of large carriers with predominantly domestic operations are preparing to operate extensive international routes in competition with the national carriers. Examples include domestic carriers in Australia, India, and Japan. In Japan, All Nippon Airways, previously a domestic carrier, has started international scheduled operations, and Toa Domestic Airlines, yet another domestic carrier, has been seeking international route authority. Similar developments are taking place with Indian Airlines, which in the past has been predominantly a domestic carrier. This trend not only will increase competition for the national carriers in international operations but will also decrease the domestic feed to other established international carriers.

The fifth area of change, though by no means restricted to this region, relates to the commercialization of government-owned airlines. As in Europe, most airlines in this region have been completely or partially owned by their governments; but the privatization movement has been gaining momentum, as evidenced by recent developments in Japan, Malaysia, Singapore, and Thailand. A reduction in government ownership will undoubtedly increase pressure on airlines to pursue objectives that are more commercially based. The privatization movement will increase airline efficiency and promote greater competition in the industry. Thus, although some carriers may not be in a position to pursue privatization or may not desire to move in this direction, they will still be affected by the operations of those carriers in the region that do become wholly or partially privatized. Not only will the privatized airlines be in a position to have access to the capital market to finance new airplane expansion programs, but their operations will undoubtedly be more efficient and more responsive to the changing needs of the marketplace instead of the government's. Unfortunately, smaller airlines and airlines operating to and from countries with less strategic geographical locations are likely to become less competitive, leading their governments to become even more protective. Even some of the large, fully developed nations are likely to continue to pursue cautious regulatory approaches if their economies depend heavily on their national carriers or if their national airlines are threatened by a loss of market share in a more competitive environment.

Of course, not all carriers can attract private capital even if they want to, and not every airline wants to take the privatization route. Only the well-managed, financially strong, and profitable (or potentially profitable) airlines can pursue flotation of common shares. An example of a large international carrier that was forced to become lean and mean in contemplation of privatization is British Airways (BA). In order to prosper as an unsubsidized carrier in the competitive marketplace, BA first had to (1) drastically reduce its labor force, (2) restructure its operations (fleet, routes, and management organizations), and (3) open its books and management decisions to public scrutiny. A number of airlines in the Asia-Pacific region either may not be in a position to fulfill these requirements or may not want to do so.

The sixth change relates to the development of airplanes with extra long-range capability. Both interregional and intraregional route structures have been affected considerably by the continuous advances in airplane technology. Before the introduction of the jet airplane, route structures in the region were dictated by the range of the piston airplane. The introduction of jet airplanes, with their higher speeds and greater range, made it feasible, for example, to fly nonstop between Japan and the U.S. West Coast. The routes to Australia made stops either at Fiji or at Tahiti and New Zealand. The intermediate stops—Honolulu in the case of Tokyo and Fiji, Tahiti and New Zealand in the case of Australia—were well suited from the point of the view of both airlines and passengers. When the B-747 was introduced, its operations were initially limited to high-density routes, such as Los Angeles–Tokyo. Carriers such as Northwest then developed extensive hub operations at Tokyo to serve beyond points. Later, the development of an even longer-range airplane (B-747SP) made it possible to fly nonstop on exceptionally long-haul routes, such as New York–Tokyo and Los Angeles–Sydney. The introduction of the standard B-747, with more powerful engines, not only matched the range performance of the B-747SP but achieved this higher performance with lower operating costs. Airplanes with very long range, lower capacity, and lower unit operating costs are constantly changing the trans-Pacific route structure between North America and the Asia-Pacific region.

Long-range airplanes with superior operating cost characteristics are also beginning to change the route structure between the Asia-Pacific region and Europe. In the past, service between Europe and some parts of Asia was provided on either a multistop or connecting basis. Flights from Tokyo, Hong Kong, and Singapore made intermediate stops in the Middle East, and flights from Australia made multiple stops on the way to Europe. During the past dozen or so years, a number of Southeast Asian airlines took advantage of intermediate stops in the Middle East to transport migrant workers. Many also exercised sixth-freedom rights to carry traffic between major points in Europe and Japan, on the one hand, and Australia, on the other. With the introduction of such airplanes as the long-range B-747, flights are now nonstop between London and Singapore, Hong Kong, and Tokyo. Although the capacity of existing wide-body airplanes limits the long-haul nonstop flights to only a few major cities in the Asia-Pacific region, the development of lower-capacity long-range airplanes (such as the MD-11 and the A-340) will eliminate the need for many intermediate stops and will allow the introduction of new service to low-density destinations in Europe, Africa, and possibly South America.

The seventh trend is the liberalization of the Soviet Union's policy, allowing access to the trans-Siberian route. Until recently, Japan Air Lines had a monopoly on the London–Tokyo nonstop route across Siberia. This service was an attractive alternative to one-stop service over Anchorage. Liberalization of the Soviet Union's policy now allows British Airways and BCAL to fly nonstop over the trans-Siberian route. This trend, coupled with British Airways' increasingly competitive posture, will further intensify competition between Europe and the Far East.

The eighth trend relates to the shift in tourism, which is now playing an important role in the economic development of a number of countries in this region. In terms of foreign exchange alone, tourism ranks first in Thailand, second in Hong Kong, third in Singapore, fourth in New Zealand, fifth in Indonesia, and seventh in Malaysia.[10] Not only are individual countries in the region expanding their activities related to tourism, but some are pushing the concept of integrated intraregional tourism. This concept embodies more than joint promotion and coordination among airlines and industry groups; it also includes multinational initiatives to develop major hub airports and resort facilities as well as direct intraregional services to and from major gateway cities. As an example of how regional services can expand tourism, Kong notes that direct air service between resort areas of southern Spain and major cities in Europe has been an important stimulus to the expansion of tourism to Spain.[11]

Route structures linking small islands in the South Pacific—the ninth trend—represent interesting opportunities in the future. These islands are spread across a vast area, from French Polynesia in the east to Papua New Guinea in the west and from the Marianas in the north to the Norfolk in the south. In the past, some of these islands depended heavily on the tourist traffic making intermediate stops between North America and Australia. Nonstop services have therefore had a significant impact on the economic viability of a number of these island nations and their national airlines. In addition to the considerations of geography and small traffic bases, air transportation services to, from, and among these islands have been subjected to a wide variety of regulations, as a result of the association of different islands to different countries, such as Australia, Britain, France, and the United States. Moreover, local airlines serving the islands have been inadequately equipped to provide the necessary services and to stimulate the traffic. For example, not only are schedules poorly integrated, but many passengers do not have access to through-fares.

The situation could change, however. First, those islands that have attained independence in recent years should be in a position to establish their own air transportation policies on the basis of their own foreign policy and economic considerations. Second, the Association of South Pacific Airlines (ASPA) has been revived to help member airlines solve their common problems through cooperation and to help them become more efficient. This association could play a critical role in the establishment of joint programs to improve the efficiency of airline operations in this region and in the development of programs to stimulate passenger traffic. Third, there is also a real possibility that a number of the island airlines could consolidate their operations, offer joint services, or have services provided by outside airlines. For example, joint ventures have been culminated between some of these islands and Ansett Airlines of Australia. Finally, it is possible that some of the islands could group together and negotiate bilateral agreements on the basis of community of interest. However, despite these positive signs, the long-term prospects for many islands are quite bleak, as a result of their lack of resources to develop viable economies and their dependence on foreign aid.

Of all the foregoing trends, liberalization, privatization, and the availability of cost-effective very long range airplanes will be most influential in intensifying competition in the marketplace. Fierce competition in both inter- and intraregional markets, in turn, could force a certain amount of consolidation, operation of joint services, or at least a rationalization of some airlines' routes, fleets, and work forces. It is conceivable, for example, that airlines that either are inefficient or have previously depended heavily on sixth-freedom traffic may be forced to regionalize their operations along the lines of SAS or Air Afrique, offer some joint services along the lines of the agreement between SABENA and BCAL, or scale down their operations along the lines of Pan American. Alternatively, they could become even more dependent on their respective governments.

Table 6–2
International City Pairs with Highest Scheduled Passenger Traffic, 1984

City Pairs	Passengers (000's)		
	→	←	Both Directions
1. London–Paris	1,060	1,105	2,165
2. London–New York	1,052	1,063	2,115
3. Kuala Lumpur–Singapore	662	654	1,316
4. Hong Kong–Tokyo	621	622	1,243
5. Amsterdam–London	560	555	1,115
6. Hong Kong–Taipei	553	561	1,114
7. Honolulu–Tokyo	521	480	1,001
8. Taipei–Tokyo	474	507	981
9. Bangkok–Hong Kong	500	453	953
10. New York–Paris	432	460	892
11. Jakarta–Singapore	442	442	884
12. Frankfurt–New York	422	430	852
13. Dublin–London	421	425	846
14. Seoul–Tokyo	424	413	837
15. Algiers–Paris	382	404	786
16. Cairo–Jidda	409	361	770
17. New York–Rome	363	405	768
18. Frankfurt–London	387	374	761
19. Hong Kong–Singapore	382	364	746
20. New York–Toronto	349	371	720
21. Bangkok–Singapore	317	368	685
22. Los Angeles–Tokyo	334	344	678
23. Miami–Nassau	333	335	668
24. Chicago–Toronto	338	318	656
25. Copenhagen–Oslo	306	298	604

Source: International Civil Aviation Organization (ICAO), *Civil Aviation Statistics of the World* (Montreal: ICAO, August 1986), 22.

Route Structure and Passenger Traffic Flows

The Asia-Pacific region contains some of the highest passenger traffic density markets in the world. In 1984, for example, Kuala Lumpur–Singapore and Hong Kong–Tokyo were the third and fourth highest density international routes in the world, as measured by the number of origin–destination passengers. Table 6–2 shows the ranking of the top twenty-five international passenger markets in the world for 1984. Six of the ten largest and eleven of the top twenty-five international routes are to, from, or within the Asia-Pacific region. During 1984, 43.3 percent of the passenger traffic was interregional (to and from this area to other regions, such as North America and Europe) and 56.3 percent was intraregional (within the area). Tables 6–3 and 6–4 show the main passenger traffic flows to, from, and within the Asia-Pacific region on all international scheduled services in 1979 and 1984. Between 1979 and 1984, the highest growth in Asia-Pacific interregional pas-

Table 6–3

Main Passenger Traffic Flows to, from, and within the Asia-Pacific Region on All International Scheduled Services, 1979 and 1984

Route Group	Number of Passengers (000)		Average Annual Growth Rate, 1979–84 (%)	Percentage Distribution	
	1979	1984		1979	1984
Interregional					
To and from Europe	5,094	6,509	5.0	16.2	14.1
To and from Middle East	2,831	5,869	15.8	9.0	12.7
To and from North America	4,853	7,152	8.0	15.5	15.4
To and from other regions	328	519	9.6	1.0	1.1
Subtotal	13,106	20,049	8.9	41.7	43.3
Intra–Asia-Pacific					
Within subregions	12,051	15,424	5.1	38.3	33.3
Between subregions	6,273	10,819	11.5	20.0	23.4
Subtotal	18,324	26,243	7.5	58.3	56.7
Total Asia-Pacific	31,430	46,292	8.0	100.0	100.0

Source: International Civil Aviation Organization (ICAO), *International Air Passenger and Freight Transport: Asia and Pacific* (Montreal: ICAO, September 1986), 51.

senger traffic was in traffic to the Middle East (15.8 percent) and the lowest growth was in traffic to Europe (5 percent). For intraregional passenger movements, the average growth rate between subregions was more than twice the average growth rate within subregions (11.5 percent versus 5.1 percent). The central and northeast subregions were the most important generators of passenger traffic, both within each subregion and between the two subregions.

Not only is the Asia-Pacific region well connected with other regions of the world, but the route network within the region is also quite extensive. In September 1985, there were more than 300 through-plane scheduled service links to countries outside the region plus more than 300 through-plane services linking the countries within the region. The most developed links, of course, are to and from North America and Europe. The least developed links are to Africa and South America. The greatest communities of interest are between the western subregion and the Middle East, between the northeastern subregion and North America, and between the central subregion and Europe. Some of these traffic flows are driven by aircraft economics and performance. Within the region, the most developed links are within the western,

Table 6–4
Passengers Carried within and between Asia-Pacific Subregions on All International Scheduled Services, 1979 and 1984

Route Group	Number of Passengers (000)		Average Annual Growth Rate 1979–84 (%)	Percentage Distribution	
	1979	1984		1979	1984
Within subregions					
Western	781	1,163	8.1	4.3	4.4
Central	5,698	7,616	6.0	31.1	29.0
Northeastern	3,619	4,681	5.3	19.7	17.9
Southeastern	1,953	1,964	0	10.7	7.5
Subtotal	12,051	15,424	5.1	65.8	58.8
Between subregions					
Central–Northeastern	4,262	7,041	10.6	23.2	26.8
Central–Southeastern	988	1,858	13.5	5.4	7.1
Central–Western	781	1,407	12.5	4.3	5.4
Southeastern–Northeastern	102	312	25.1	0.5	1.2
Western–Northeastern	104	139	6.0	0.6	0.5
Western–Southeastern	36	62	11.5	0.2	0.2
Subtotal	6,273	10,819	11.5	34.2	41.2
Total intra–Asia-Pacific	18,324	26,243	7.5	100.0	100.0

Source: International Civil Aviation Organization (ICAO), *International Air Passenger and Freight Transport: Asia and Pacific* (Montreal: ICAO, September 1986), 53.

central, and northeastern subregions; the least developed links are between the southeastern and western subregions.

In 1984, 15.4 percent of the total Asia-Pacific international scheduled passenger traffic (35.7 percent of the total traffic moving between the Asia-Pacific region and all other regions) moved to and from North America. And the lion's share of this traffic either originated from or was destined for the United States. More specifically, the largest component of this traffic was between the United States and the Asian Pacific Rim countries, and most of this traffic has traditionally moved over Japan. Indeed, two-thirds of all traffic between the Asia-Pacific region and North America has been travel to and from the northeast subregion. Some of the flights from the United States that did bypass Tokyo did so because of the frequency limitations implemented by the Japanese, partly to protect the national carrier and partly because of capacity limitations of the international airport at Tokyo.

Despite its spectacular growth, the trans-Pacific market is still relatively small compared to other major international markets. In terms of passengers, in 1985, the North America–Far East market (3.5 million passengers) and the North America–Southwest Pacific market (1.2 million passengers) combined were only 7.8 percent of the size of the intra-European market, 26 percent of the North America–Europe market, and only 2.9 percent of all origin–destination traffic. In addition, interregional traffic between the Far East and the Southwest Pacific accounted for just 1.3 percent of all origin–destination traffic, and all traffic within these two regions represented a mere 5.2 percent of worldwide origin–destination traffic (see table 6–5). Even in terms of passenger-kilometers flown (which takes into account the much greater distances for the trans-Pacific markets), the North Pacific, Mid Pacific, and South Pacific markets combined (43 million passenger-kilometers) are smaller than the intra-European markets (55 million passenger-kilometers), which involve much shorter stage lengths, and much smaller than the North Atlantic market (132 million passenger-kilometers), which also involves shorter stage lengths. The Far East subregion listed in table 6–5 includes the Indian subcontinent, Southeast Asia, and Northeast Asia. The Southwest Pacific subregion includes Australia, New Zealand, and most of the islands in this subregion.

During the past fifteen years, the average annual growth rate for total trans-Pacific passenger traffic (North, Central, and South Pacific) exceeded the trans-Atlantic rate. This differential in growth was particularly significant during the first half of the 1970s, as compared to the second half. During the first half of the 1980s, however, the average annual growth in the North America–Far East passenger market was actually 1.2 percentage points *below* the growth in the North America–Europe market and only half of one percentage point above the average for all regions combined (see table 6–5). Consequently, the overall growth in the trans-Pacific markets seems to have tapered off to levels reflecting more mature markets, like the trans-Atlantic market.

Fares

In general, passenger fares in the Asia-Pacific region are developed outside the IATA traffic conference machinery. Only twelve of the forty-three international airlines based in this region participate in the IATA traffic conference machinery.[12] The Japanese market is an exception. First, this market is so dominant that it has been a controlled environment. Second, the restriction on capacity coupled with Pan American's weakness and inability to expand capacity had a significant influence on fares. To the extent that fares are coordinated, the process is achieved through the Orient Airlines Association (OAA); otherwise, they are set by individual airlines. It is important to realize

Table 6–5
IATA International On-Flight Origin and Destination Traffic
Statistics, 1980–85

Region Pair	Passengers (000), 1985	Average Annual Changes, 1980–85 (%)
North America–Middle America	9,739	0.4
North America–South America	2,622	−5.3
North America–Middle East	852	11.4
North America–Europe	17,881	4.5
North America–Africa	325	5.3
North America–Far East	3,483	3.3
North America–Southwest Pacific	1,170	−1.1
Within North America	5,650	−1.1
Middle America–South America	608	−3.6
Middle America–Middle East	—	—
Middle America–Europe	1,130	9.0
Middle America–Africa	6	−25.8
Middle America–Far East	17	−1.4
Middle America–Southwest Pacific	—	—
Within Middle America	938	−4.2
South America–Middle East	11	80.2
South America–Europe	1,830	1.2
South America–Africa	83	−0.7
South America–Far East	51	13.9
South America–Southwest Pacific	29	8.3
Within South America	2,050	−6.3
Middle East–Europe	6,672	2.7
Middle East–Africa	4,366	4.6
Middle East–Far East	5,288	10.1
Middle East–Southwest Pacific	23	10.6
Within Middle East	5,058	4.2
Europe–Africa	13,893	3.9
Europe–Far East	3,936	5.6
Europe–Southwest Pacific	741	−3.0
Within Europe	59,910	2.7
Africa–Far East	338	4.4
Africa–Southwest Pacific	44	−3.4
Within Africa	3,005	2.3
Far East–Southwest Pacific	2,167	8.4
Within Far East	6,359	6.9
Within Southwest Pacific	2,143	1.4
TOTAL OFOD–All services	162,418	2.8%

Source: International Air Transport Association (IATA), World Air Transport Statistics (Geneva: IATA, June 1986), 30.

Table 6–6

Comparison of Average Normal Economy Fares per Passenger-Kilometer in the Asia-Pacific Region, September 1985

Route Group	Cents/Kilometer by Distance (km)							
	250	500	1,000	2,000	4,000	8,000	12,000	16,000
Asia-Pacific	18.2	16.3	14.6	13.0	11.7	10.4	9.8	—
Europe–Asia-Pacific	—	—	18.3	15.6	13.2	11.2	10.2	9.5
North–Mid Pacific	—	—	—	—	12.1	9.8	8.6	7.9
South Pacific	—	—	—	—	14.8	12.2	11.0	10.1
Int'l total–World	28.7	23.6	19.4	16.0	13.2	10.8	9.7	8.9

Source: International Civil Aviation Organization (ICAO), *Survey of International Air Transport Fares and Rates, September 1985* (Montreal: ICAO, June 1986).

that unlike the IATA, the OAA has neither an official fare-making function nor recognition in bilateral agreements. It is simply an informal forum for fare discussions. Thus, fares are set by individual airlines and are subject to the approval of the relevant governments under bilateral agreements. And it is generally well known that there is widespread discounting (undercutting government-approved fares) from the published fares, even though the OAA supposedly has programs that promote fare integrity.

In the past, most of the countries in this region have promoted bilateral agreements containing "double approval" fare clauses, which require government approval from both bilateral partners. In recent years, a variety of approaches to tariff regulation have been implemented in the bilateral agreements. Some countries, such as Australia, have promoted the "country of origin" pricing scheme, which allows the governments of each country to control tariffs applicable to traffic originating in that country; some others, such as Singapore, have promoted the "double disapproval" approach, which requires that the governments of both partners disapprove a tariff to prevent it from being implemented; still others, such as China, have promoted the "zone of reasonableness" approach, under which a fare that falls within an agreed-upon range receives automatic approval. It should be emphasized, however, that very few governments in this region scrutinize the tariffs filed by their carriers.

Table 6–6 shows (for September 1985) the variation in published average normal economy fares per kilometer for selected route groups involving the Asia-Pacific region. Before examining these fares and comparing them with those in other regions in the world, it is necessary to keep in mind not only that there is widespread discounting from these published fares but that there are many types of special fares 50 percent or more below the level of normal economy fares. Compared to other regions in the world, the published fares over comparable distances were higher than the world average for travel between this region and the South Pacific. For intraregional travel on the whole, normal economy fares were lower than the world average, taking into account the difference in distances. In general, fares were also lower than the world average for travel on the North Pacific and Mid Pacific and between Europe and the Asia-Pacific region. Directional variations in fares exist as a result of fluctuations in currencies. There is a wide variation among airlines in the distribution of passenger traffic by type of fare. Socioeconomic characteristics of the markets, the availability of sophisticated yield-management systems, marketing policies and route structures of individual airlines, and the level and type of competition are some of the factors that account for this variation in the passenger traffic distribution by fare type.

Financial Performance

The overall financial performance of the scheduled airlines based in the Asia-Pacific region during the past ten years has been superior to the performance of airlines based in other parts of the world. Tables 6–7 and 6–8 show financial results and operating revenues, respectively, for the scheduled airlines based in the Asia-Pacific region in comparison to all scheduled airlines in 1974, 1979, and 1984. In general, revenues have increased at a faster rate than costs. The airlines as a group are more profitable on an operating basis and on a net basis (that is, after nonoperating costs). The superior financial performance of the Asia-Pacific carriers is partly due to higher growth in both passenger and freight traffic and partly due to the lower increase in unit operating costs compared to the average increase for all airlines.

Table 6–9 shows the increase in various components of unit operating costs for the airlines in this region compared to all airlines. Airlines based in the Asia-Pacific region seem to have more financial advantages than disadvantages. During the ten years between 1974 and 1984, the increase in total operating costs for the Asia-Pacific carriers was lower than the world average. These carriers enjoy lower labor costs and higher labor productivity, which have offset higher unit operating costs for fuel and depreciation. Traditionally, airlines that belong to the smaller nations in this area have claimed that their inventory holding costs are higher than those of the airlines in Europe and North America.[13] This situation is being rectified by increasing cooperation among airlines in such technical areas as maintenance and training. A good example is the revival of ASPA to increase cooperation among the island airlines in the South Pacific.

The Asia-Pacific airlines also benefit significantly from the greater proportion of wide-body airplanes in their fleets. Although the acquisition of these airplanes raised unit depreciation and amortization expenses, it also

Table 6–7
Financial Results of Scheduled Airlines, Asia-Pacific and World, 1974, 1979, and 1984
(*U.S. $, millions*)

Item	Asia-Pacific Region			World		
	1974	*1979*	*1984*	*1974*	*1979*	*1984*
Total operating revenues	3,900	10,600	18,200	33,080	70,750	104,800
Total operating expenses	3,900	10,280	17,000	32,290	70,020	99,700
Operating result	0	320	1,200	790	730	5,100
Net result	−60	120	560	40	590	2,000
Expressed as percentage of total operating revenues						
Operating result	0	3.0%	6.6%	2.4%	1.0%	4.9%
Net result	−1.5%	1.1%	3.1%	0.1%	0.8%	1.9%

Source: International Civil Aviation Organization (ICAO), *International Air Passenger and Freight Transport: Asia and Pacific* (Montreal: ICAO, September 1986), 83.

Table 6–8
Operating Revenues of Asia-Pacific Scheduled Airlines, 1974, 1979,
and 1984

| Revenue Source | U.S.$ (millions) | | | Average Annual Growth Rates (%) | | | | | |
| | | | | Airlines of the Region | | | World | | |
	1974	1979	1984	1974–79	1979–84	1974–84	1974–79	1979–84	1974–84
Scheduled services									
Passenger	3,130	8,470	14,040	22.0	10.6	16.2	17.1	7.6	12.2
Freight	430	1,360	2,770	25.9	15.3	20.5	16.4	10.1	13.2
Mail	80	140	240	11.8	11.4	11.6	9.6	5.6	7.6
Total scheduled	3,640	9,970	17,050	22.3	11.3	16.7	16.8	7.8	12.2
Nonscheduled flights	110	180	350	10.4	14.2	12.3	10.8	3.7	7.2
Incidental revenues	150	450	800	24.6	12.2	18.2	17.2	17.1	17.1
Total operating revenues	3,900	10,600	18,200	22.1	11.4	16.7	16.6	8.2	12.3

Source: International Civil Aviation Organization (ICAO), International Air Passenger and Freight Transport: Asia and Pacific (Montreal: ICAO, September 1986), 83.

Table 6–9
Unit Operating Expenses of Asia-Pacific Scheduled Airlines Compared with the World Average, 1974, 1979, and 1984

Item	Operating Expenses per Ton-Kilometer Available (U.S. cents)			Growth Rate (%)		
	1974	1979	1984	1974–79	1979–84	1974–84
Flight operations less fuel and oil						
Asia/Pacific	3.0	2.8	3.1	– 1.4	2.1	0.3
World	3.0	3.8	4.0	4.8	1.0	2.9
Fuel and oil						
Asia/Pacific	5.1	9.4	10.2	13.0	1.6	7.2
World	4.3	8.0	9.3	13.2	3.1	8.0
Maintenance and overhaul						
Asia/Pacific	2.8	3.8	3.6	6.3	– 1.1	2.5
World	2.9	3.9	4.0	6.1	0.5	3.3
Depreciation and amortization						
Asia/Pacific	2.8	3.0	4.1	1.4	6.4	3.9
World	1.9	2.3	2.9	3.9	4.7	4.3
User charges and station expenses						
Asia/Pacific	3.7	5.6	5.9	8.6	1.0	4.8
World	3.9	5.9	6.4	8.6	1.6	5.1
Passenger services						
Asia/Pacific	2.4	3.4	3.3	7.2	– 0 6	3.2
World	2.2	3.3	3.7	8.4	2.3	5.3
Ticketing, sales, and promotion						
Asia/Pacific	4.1	6.1	6.6	8.3	1.6	4.9
World	3.2	5.2	6.6	10.2	4.9	7.5
General, administrative, and others						
Asia/Pacific	1.2	1.6	1.6	5.9	0.0	2.9
World	1.4	2.1	3.0	8.4	7.4	7.9
Total operating expenses						
Asia/Pacific	25.1	35.7	38.4	7.3	1.5	4.3
World	22.7	34.5	39.9	8.7	3.0	5.8

Source: International Civil Aviation Organization (ICAO), *International Air Passenger and Freight Transport: Asia and Pacific* (Montreal: ICAO, September 1986), 89.

provided lower unit operating costs relative to the unit costs of operating either narrow-body equipment or earlier models of wide-body equipment. As of the end of 1986, almost 50 percent of the fleets operated by carriers based in the Asia-Pacific region consisted of wide-body airplanes, whereas in 1979, wide-body airplanes represented less than 20 percent of the region's fleets.

It is interesting to note that profitable operations have allowed this region's carriers to acquire the most modern and most productive airplanes available. In turn, these modern fleets have contributed significantly to the continued profitability of operations. Singapore Airlines is the classic example of an airline that is determined to keep its fleet modern. The average age of the airline's fleet is less than three years. Of course, the government's tax policies have had a significant influence on the airline's fleet modernization program. Still, although many factors have contributed to the profitability of Singapore Airlines, rapid equipment turnover (to keep the fleet modern) has played a key role not only in keeping unit operating costs low but also in providing important marketing advantages on long-haul routes. Moreover, lower operating costs and, in turn, aggressive pricing policies (not just marketing flair) have contributed to the gain in the market share of the Asian airlines that have recently entered the marketplace. Korean, Singapore, and Chinese airlines now carry a significant portion of the trans-Pacific traffic, and their gain has been at the expense of the U.S. carriers as well as Japan Air Lines.

Future Prospects

Although the trans-Pacific market has experienced spectacular growth in the past as a result of dynamic growth in trade activity and the resultant emergence of world-class airlines, it is inappropriate to make trend-line extrapolations of such growth patterns. The Asia-Pacific region is characterized by resilient economies with above-average growth potential, and the airlines in this region will benefit from such growth. It is important to keep in mind, however, (1) that the region's air transportation market is still relatively small compared to other major international markets; (2) that the overall growth in this market seems to have tapered off to a level more reflective of the growth in mature markets; and (3) that U.S. and European protectionist inclinations may affect the region's economic growth and, hence, the growth of carriers based in this region. It is therefore unlikely that the Asia-Pacific region will become a mass market similar to the trans-Atlantic market. This conclusion is further supported by the fact that despite the availability of substantial discounts from the official fares, average fares for discretionary travelers are still fairly high. In addition, the strength of the Japanese yen has made nonbusiness travel to Japan almost prohibitive. Consequently, the bread-and-butter market will continue to be made up of business travelers. As for China, even if tourist travel continues to increase at a rapid rate, the size of the market is so small that the impact on the total market will be negligible for a number of years.

Improvements in airplane technology will continue to change the shape of the route structures in the Pacific. The development of new airplanes, with lower capacity and higher range, will have a further impact on the route structures. For example, the recently launched MD-11 will make it cost-effective to fly nonstop from the United States to a number of lower-density cities in the Far East (and Australia) and from those cities to major capitals in Europe. In the past, some stops in the Middle East were required either because of the limited range of the airplane or because of the need to pick up additional traffic at intermediate points. New-technology airplanes will also increase the possibility of more direct service to Africa and South America. In the past, LanChile provided a link between Santiago and Tahiti via Easter Island. More recently, Aerolineas Argentinas has shown interest in a new route. New-generation airplanes could play an important role in developing such new routes and stimulating traffic.

The development of new-technology airplanes, though beneficial for stimulating traffic growth to, from, and within the Asia-Pacific region (given the long stage lengths), will put more pressure on the airlines to adapt the equipment to the amount of traffic, rather than the other way around, and will provide a competitive edge for carriers in a position to acquire such airplanes. The value of a modern fleet is demonstrated quite well from (1) the experience of Pan American, a carrier that ended up abandoning its trans-Pacific operations, partly because of its inability to acquire the appropriate new airplanes; and (2) the experience of Singapore Airlines, which has consistently outperformed its competitors and is now well positioned to capitalize on the new-technology airplanes because of the higher profitability of their operations.

Finally, even if the Pacific markets continue to grow at rates slightly above the world average, profits are likely to be marginal, at least in the short term, given the emerging level of competition as a result of increasing liberalization, the privatization trend, the availability of new-technology airplanes with exceptionally long nonstop range, and the development of hubs in Bangkok, Manila, and Hong Kong, to compete with the one in Singapore. Overcapacity, coupled with a cutthroat competitive market environment, will keep load factors and fares at the marginally profitable level. As in other regions of the world, selected carriers face the prospect of minimal rates of return, which will put pressure on those airlines and their governments to scale down operations, consolidate, offer joint services, or diversify trading patterns within the region.

Notes

1. Congressional Research Service, "Economic Changes in the Asian Pacific Rim: Policy Prospectus" (Library of Congress, Congressional Research Service, Economics Division, Foreign Affairs and National Defense Division, Office of Senior Specialists, August 1986).

2. International Civil Aviation Organization (ICAO), *Air Passenger and Freight Transport: Asia and Pacific* (Montreal: ICAO, 1986), 3.

3. Ibid., 1–6.

4. Ibid., 3.

5. Joan Feldman, "Pacific Nations Ease Regulatory Grip: Deregulation Changes the Region's Competition," *Travel Weekly*, 22 September 1986, 62.

6. Teruo Sakamoto, "Factors Impacting Far East/Pacific Air Travel Demand," *Twelfth Annual FAA Aviation Forecast Conference Proceedings* (Washington, D.C.: FAA, February 1987), 78–88.

7. Dori Jones Yang, "Direct Elections in Hong Kong? Not If Beijing Can Help It," *Business Week*, 16 March 1987, 62.

8. Far Eastern Economic Review, *Asia 1987 Year Book* (Hong Kong: Far Eastern Economic Review, 1987), 188–90.

9. ICAO, *Air Passenger and Freight Transport*, 36–37.

10. Cheong Choong Kong, "Tourism, Liberalization and Low Fares Spur Asia/Pacific Region Growth," *Airport Forum*, April 1986, 48.

11. Ibid.

12. ICAO, *Air Passenger and Freight Transport*, 73.

13. Kong, "Tourism," 46.

7
Meeting the Challenges

The preceding six chapters have highlighted the nature and direction of internal and external changes in the international airline industry and the major issues and challenges facing this industry. The internal changes relate to such trends as liberalization, privatization, the increased use of automation, legitimization of gray market fares, and the availability of advanced-technology airplanes. The external changes relate to economic, financial, and political policies, on the one hand, and the changing nature of the demand for air transportation services, on the other. It must be emphasized that although changes in economic, financial, and political policies are not new, the extent to which recent developments will affect the international airline industry is unprecedented. The changing nature of the demand for air transportation services relates to the fact that leisure travel is now the dominant component of the total market on most international routes. Leisure travel has replaced business travel as the primary source of demand, with corresponding implications for airline pricing, scheduling, and product offering.

One other external trend that is affecting the airline industry (both international and domestic) is the "internationalization" of world aviation. Changes in one region are now having an impact on other regions much more quickly, as exemplified by the spread of regulatory liberalization and privatization across continents and oceans. And it is the internationalization trend that is forcing nations and airlines in all regions of the world to rethink their aviation policies and to review the structure and performance of airlines in response to the changing environment. Moreover, the gradual development of a global economy has resulted in greater interdependence; therefore, differences in regional economic growth rates will diminish with a corresponding impact on the regional growth in the demand for air transportation services. Consequently, airlines in such regions as the Middle East now face a challenge of making some painful adjustments to match capacity with realistically sustainable long-term growth in traffic.

The challenge facing airline managements and government officials responsible for the aviation sectors of their economies in five of the six ICAO regions is how to cope with new pressures on traditional philosophies. In North America, the challenge faced by airline managers is to operate their businesses according to the forces of the free marketplace in an environment in which two of the three components of air transportation—airports and the air traffic control system—continue to be controlled by the federal government.

In many parts of the world, an international airline continues to be viewed as an instrument of national policy. As such, an airline is often used to promote tourism, to earn foreign exchange, to provide essential communications, and to support national defense. For reasons of national policy, governments have not only owned their flag carriers, they have also protected them by regulating entry, capacity, and tariffs. However, international airlines in these regions have paid a price for government ownership, government protection, and a privileged status. For example, at many airlines, decisions on employment policies, capital financing, equipment orders, and routes are made by civil servants rather than by airline managers. Unfortunately, civil servants tend to respond to political and administrative priorities and constraints, whereas corporate managers are trained to respond to the needs and timing of the marketplace. However, in today's environment, government officials must continuously evaluate the costs and benefits of a state-owned airline and the government's role in the regulation, management, and operation of such an endeavor in the rapidly changing marketplace. The airlines, in turn, must plan for the changing attitudes of governments and for developments in the marketplace (both in their own regions and in other regions). For example, the recently announced merger between British Airways and BCAL will increase the pressure to liberalize within Europe and solidify the need to attain a critical mass to survive in the new environment.

An effective response to the changes in the marketplace will require a strategic marketing orientation, a full exploitation of automation (or information technology), a focus on the bottom line, and a government policy that is attuned to the changing environment. A strategic marketing orientation will require emphasis on four other elements: a long-term outlook, a conscious effort directed at spotting market opportunities, an examination of all resources (including tangible assets, labor, product attributes, route network, market information, and infrastructure), and an emphasis on flexibility. The exploitation of automation requires much more than just a commitment of resources; it requires a change in attitudes toward information technology. Successful airline managers must identify data requirements and the means of obtaining that information. A bottom line perspective ensures the implementation of rational and cost-effective strategies, and it is valid for both privately owned and government-owned airlines. Finally, governments in some regions, particularly in developing regions, should reexamine the role of their airlines. There has to be a careful assessment of the costs and benefits of greater autonomy and the degree to which government support will continue to be provided.

The pressures on governments for change have come from different sources. In the developed regions, the forces for change have come from consumers and from the changing character of the airline industry in other regions, as exemplified by the actions in North America and the reactions in Europe. In the developing regions, the forces for change have come from the changing nature of their regional economies, from the pressing demands of other sectors of their economies, and through the domino effect of developments in other regions. For example, the collapse in oil prices has forced some carriers in the Middle East to reevaluate their growth plans and to implement severe cost-reduction programs. The implementation of noise regulations by the developed countries has made a large percentage of the fleets operated by airlines in Africa and South America obsolete. The inability of countries in the Latin America/Caribbean region to service foreign debt has strained the financing capacity of the airlines based in this region to the point that they cannot obtain the necessary equipment to continue service in existing markets, let alone to expand into new markets. And finally, right or wrong (considering that the jury is still out on the *long-term total* costs and benefits of deregulation), the changing character of the U.S. international airline industry is forcing European airlines to reconfigure their resources, which is causing airlines in the Middle East, Africa, and the Asia-Pacific region to reexamine their own resources and strategies to survive in the new marketplace.

To cope with the nature and extent of changes in the external environment, both governments and airlines must examine some critical issues. In developing regions, for example, though painful, it is necessary to ask whether each and every developing nation can justify maintenance of a flag carrier on the basis of direct and indirect cost-benefit analysis. Alternatively, what are the advantages and disadvantages for a nation and its airline to be a partner in a multinational entity? At the airline level, managements not only have to remain flexible to adjust to any change in national policy, but they have to balance the realities of the marketplace with the goals of governments in a cost-effective manner. In developed regions, on the other hand, the focus is on the marketplace and the bottom line. In these regions, market-led planning, which relies on the availability and utilization of market research, is not just fashionable now, it has become imperative. Well-positioned airlines are creating whole new departments whose primary responsibility is to explore new opportunities and to find cost-effective means of capitalizing on these opportunities. For example, the changing trade patterns of countries in Southeast Asia are representing new opportunities for airlines to diversify their capacity.

In addition to the need for strategic market orientation and an emphasis on flexibility, airlines have to capitalize on the benefits of automation. Automation, which was once simply a tool to reduce costs by increasing operational efficiency and telecommunications (which meant either telephone lines or links to reservation computers), is now also a managerial tool to help solve the airline industry's most critical problem—its inability to match supply with demand. This is a unique industry; despite growth in air travel demand well in excess of growth in the GNP, despite continuous reductions in operating costs as a result of high-productivity airplanes, and despite government protection from excessive competition, the industry's aggregate return on investment has been marginal. The single most important cause of this problem has been the lack of harmonization between supply and demand. Computerized reservation systems, coupled with data networks providing critical information in a timely manner, are proving to be extremely valuable in solving this problem through cost-effective market segmentation and pricing and yield management. Furthermore, automation is proving to be effective in product development, distribution, and even product differentiation. The competitive advantages enjoyed by American and United in the United States, resulting from the use of information technology, have been well publicized. Other examples of innovative use of information technology include SAS, which began to check passenger baggage and issue boarding passes when customers checked out of their hotels, and the implementation of frequent flyer programs to build brand loyalty. Automation could also play an integral role in the legitimization of under-the-table fares, which has become an important rationalization for the liberalization of airline pricing policies in some regions.

Regrettably, there are airlines at the other end of the spectrum that have not even begun to understand the benefit of information technology, let alone exploit it. Benefiting from the use of automation does not necessarily imply that each international airline has to follow the lead of sophisticated airlines or commit substantial resources. In many developing airlines, the use of an affordable stand-alone microcomputer, coupled with an understanding of its application to airline management, could reduce operating costs, enhance revenue, and improve the quality of service provided to customers.

It is obvious that the changing environment worldwide has produced challenges for the management of international airlines. Although the new environment contains substantial risks, it also presents enormous opportunities. At the government level, officials responsible for a flag carrier must assess the contributions and liabilities of their national airline, the role of their national carrier, and their own role in the general management and operations of that airline. Senior airline managers, for their part, (1) must mobilize their airline organizations to meet accelerating change, which must be looked upon not as a problem but as a responsibility and an opportunity; and (2) must shift the focus of debates on the liberalization movement and the implementation of information technology from constraints to opportunities. The challenge for planners is to reconfigure and redeploy their airlines' resources, with built-in flexibility, by capitalizing on their airlines' and their nations' structural strengths. Finally, for airline marketing organizations, the challenge is to broaden their horizon from passive thinking to adaptive thinking and, ultimately, to creative thinking to respond effectively to the consumerism movement in the developed economies and to resource constraints and barriers to progress in the developing economies.

Bibliography

Association of European Airlines (AEA). *Yearbook 1986*. Brussels: AEA, May 1987.
———. *EEC Air Transport Policy: AEA Views*. Brussels: AEA, July 1984.
Brenner, M.A., J.O. Leet, and E. Schott. *Airline Deregulation*. Westport, Conn.: ENO Foundation for Transportation, 1985.
Commission of the European Communities. *Contributions of the European Communities to the Development of Air Transport Service: Memorandum to the Commission*. Brussels: EEC, 6 July 1979.
———. *Civil Aviation Memorandum No. 2: Progress Towards the Development of a Community Air Transport Policy*. Brussels: EEC, 15 March, 1984.
Congressional Research Service. "Economic Changes in the Asian Pacific Rim: Policy Prospectus." Library of Congress, Congressional Research Service, Economics Division, Foreign Affairs and National Defense Division, Office of Senior Specialists, August 1986.
Doganis, Rigas. *Flying Off Course: The Economics of International Airlines*. London: George Allen & Unwin, 1985.
Endres, Gunter G. *World Airline Fleets*. London: Aviation Data Centre, 1986.
Europa. *The Europa Year Book 1986*. London: Europa Publications, 1986.
———. *Africa: South of the Sahara, 1987*, 16th ed. London: Europa Publications, 1987.
Far Eastern Economic Review. *Asia 1987 Year Book*. Hong Kong: Far Eastern Economic Review, 1987.
Hopkins, Jack W., ed. *Latin America and Caribbean Contemporary Record*. Vol. IV. New York: Holmes and Meier, 1986.
International Air Transport Association (IATA). *Commercial Aviation in Developing Countries*. Geneva: IATA, June 1982.
———. *Future Challenges in African Air Transport*. Geneva: IATA, June 1985.
———. "Workable Competition: The Emerging Market Environment." An aviation seminar held in Puerto Azul, Philippines, 20–22 September 1985.
———. *World Air Transport Statistics, 1985*. Geneva: IATA, June 1986.
International Civil Aviation Organization (ICAO). *Middle East: International Air Passenger and Freight Transport*. Montreal: ICAO, January 1982.
———. *International Air Passenger and Freight Transport: Latin America and the Caribbean*. Montreal: ICAO, May 1983.

———. *International Air Passenger and Freight Transport: Africa.* Montreal: ICAO, March 1985.

———. *Bulletin.* Montreal: ICAO, June 1986.

———. *Survey of International Air Transport Fares and Rates, September 1985.* Montreal: ICAO, June 1986.

———. *Regional Differences in Fares, Rates and Costs for International Air Transport.* Montreal: ICAO, July 1986.

———. *The Economic Situation of Air Transport: Review and Outlook.* Montreal: ICAO, July 1986.

———. *Civil Aviation Statistics of the World.* Montreal: ICAO, August 1986.

———. *Air Passenger and Freight Transport: Asia and Pacific.* Montreal: ICAO, September 1986.

———. *Traffic by Flight Stage.* Montreal: ICAO, December 1986.

———. *Financial Data.* Montreal: ICAO, December 1986.

Japan Transport Consultants Association (JTCA). *Information Booklet (1985): Outline of Civil Aviation in Japan.* Tokyo: JTCA, 1986.

Keen, Peter G.W. *Competing in Time: Using Telecommunications for Competitive Advantage.* Cambridge, Mass.: Ballinger, 1986.

Sakamoto, Teruo. "Factors Impacting Far East/Pacific Air Travel Demand." *Twelfth Annual FAA Aviation Forecast Conference Proceedings.* Washington, D.C.: FAA, February 1987.

Shaw, S. *Airline Marketing and Management.* 2nd ed. London: Pitman, 1985.

Taneja, Nawal K. *International Aviation Policy.* Lexington, Mass.: Lexington Books, 1980.

———. *Airline Planning: Corporate, Financial, and Marketing.* Lexington, Mass.: Lexington Books, 1982.

The Economist Intelligence Unit. *International Tourism Quarterly.* Report No. 4. London: The Economist, 1985.

The Economist Publications. *International Tourism Reports.* Report No. 2. London: The Economist, May 1986.

———. *International Tourism Reports.* Report No. 4. London: The Economist, November 1986.

Thomas, Rubel. "Factors Impacting Latin American Air Travel Demand." *Twelfth Annual FAA Aviation Forecast Conference Proceedings.* Washington, D.C.: FAA, February 1987.

Western Transportation Advisory Council (WTAC). "The Canada-U.S. Treaty Is Particularly Important," *WESTAC Newsletter,* Vol. 12, No. 4. Vancouver, B.C.: WTAC, October 1986.

Wheatcroft, Stephen, and Geoffrey Lipman. *Air Transport in a Competitive European Market.* London: The Economist, 1986.

World Tourism Organization (WTO). *Compendium of Tourism Statistics.* Madrid: WTO, 1986.

Index

Index

About the Author

Nawal K. Taneja is a professor at The Ohio State University, in the Department of Aviation in the School of Engineering and the Marketing Department in the School of Business. Prior to this position, he was president and chief executive officer of an airline that operated jet equipment, president of a research firm that provided consulting services to the worldwide aviation community, associate professor in the Flight Transportation Division of the Department of Aeronautics and Astronautics at the Massachusetts Institute of Technology, and senior economic analyst with Trans World Airlines. At OSU, Dr. Taneja teaches and conducts research in airline analysis and planning. He is the author of seven other books on the airline industry. Dr. Taneja is a consultant to airlines, airport authorities, aircraft manufacturers, and government organizations throughout the world.